YANKEE DOODLE WENT to CHURCH

YANKEE DOODLE WENT TO CHURCH

JAMES L. ADAMS

Fleming H. Revell Company
Old Tappan, New Jersey

Scripture quotations in this volume are from the King James Version of the Bible.

Quotations from MITRE AND SCEPTRE by Carl Bridenbaugh used by permission of Oxford University Press.

Reprinted by permission of Charles Scribner's Sons, an imprint of Macmillan Publishing Company from RELIGION IN COLONIAL AMERICA by William Warren Sweet. Copyright 1942 Charles Scribner's Sons; copyright renewed © 1970 William Warren Sweet, Jr.

Quotations from PETER OLIVER'S ORIGIN AND PROGRESS OF THE AMERICAN REBELLION, edited by Douglass Adair and John A. Schutz reprinted by permission of The Henry E. Huntington Library and Art Gallery.

Quotations from A RELIGIOUS HISTORY OF THE AMERICAN PEOPLE by Sydney E. Ahlstrom used by permission of Yale University Press, © 1972 by Sydney E. Ahlstom.

Quotations from ERRAND INTO THE WILDERNESS by Perry Miller reprinted by permission of Belknap Press.

Quotations from RELIGION AND THE AMERICAN MIND by Alan Heimert reprinted by permission of Harvard University Press.

Exerpts from THE STORY OF RELIGION IN AMERICA by William Warren Sweet, Harper & Row, 1930, 1939, 1950. Harper & Row Publishers, Inc. Reprinted by permission of the publisher.

Library of Congress Cataloging-in-Publication Data

Adams, James L. (James Lewis), date
    Yankee Doodle went to church.

    Bibliography: p.
    1. United States—History—Revolution, 1775–1783—Religious aspects.
2. Church and state—United States—History—18th century.   3. United
States—Church history—Colonial period, ca. 1600–1775.   I. Title.
E209.A33   1989   973.3′8   88-31814
ISBN 0-8007-1619-1

Copyright © 1989 by James L. Adams
Published by the Fleming H. Revell Company
Old Tappan, New Jersey 07675
Printed in the United States of America

CONTENTS

TO Jamie, my son,
Caitlin, granddaughter number one,
and
Cheryl Lynn, the spark

Acknowledgments

This book grew out of a conversation I had with fellow religion writer Dick Ostling, of *Time* magazine, in the early 1970s. We were covering a national church convention in my home city of Cincinnati. The denomination was split on what stand to take on the Vietnam War—a question troubling millions of Americans at the time. It was also the era when liberation theology crossed the Mexican border and made its way into the columns of United States church magazines.

During the course of our conversation, Dick and I discussed the stance of the evangelical Puritan clergy during the American Revolution. We wondered how eighteenth-century evangelical Christians, with their high view of Scripture, supported the Revolution of '76. How did they justify it from a biblical point of view? What about the loyalists? Did they use the Word to support the Tory position?

An attempt to get the answers to those questions sent me on a five-year quest of reading history books, magazine articles, pamphlets, and interviewing any historian coming to town to make a speech or attend a seminar.

Let me state at the outset that I am neither a historian nor a theologian. This is not a scholarly treatise based on original research. As a newspaperman with thirty-five years' experience, I approached writing a book in the same manner I would had I been given an assignment by the city desk. I picked the brains of others, both the living and the dead, who were kind enough to put their thoughts into writing. I found during my research that many of the authors quoted the same sources. So in that sense, at least, journalists and historians are alike. I have tried to give my sources credit in the source notes. If I have quoted some author without acknowledging it, please mark it up as an inadvertent error.

Much of this manuscript was finished by 1976, and it lay in state in my basement for several years. During that time portions appeared in the *Cincinnati Post* in my weekly religious column "A Layman's View." Under the prodding of my daughter, Cheryl Lynn Roedel, I resurrected the manuscript, refurbished it, and Cheryl retyped it. I am grateful for her gadfly role as well as her expertise on the word processor. My thanks also to my sister, June Adams, who typed the original and also parts of the revised version. In addition I owe a debt of gratitude to the Cincinnati Public Library, where I did much of my research, which gave me special privileges to the materials in its rare-book department.

Editors are seldom lauded by authors they pick on, but I am especially grateful to Dr. Mark A. Noll, Wheaton College history professor and an author himself, for his careful reading of my manuscript and his pointed comments that helped sharpen my focus.

But without the Fleming H. Revell Publishing Company, this book, like many a rose, would have "blushed unseen and wasted its fragrance in the desert air." So thanks, Revell.

INTRODUCTION

Freedom's Religious Roots

Freedom was not born a bastard. It was birthed in blood during the American Revolution, when church and state were still married. Separation would come later. The Founding Fathers called only for separation—not divorce. Only in the latter half of this century has the United States Supreme Court held that church and state should be legally divorced. As a result of having its religious roots cut out from under it, freedom currently suffers from an identity crisis.

Seventeenth-century Puritan New England saw the state as the church's enforcer. The church set the standards, and the state policed them. That included requiring nonchurch members to pay taxes or tithes to the established church, attend services or be penalized, and to keep the Sabbath. Some states—including Puritan Massachusetts and Anglican Virginia—permitted only church members to hold public office.

On that warm April morning in 1775, when the first shots of the Revolution were fired on a church green in Lexington, Massachusetts, nine of the thirteen colonies had established churches. After the Revolution, the church-state roles gradually reversed, but the original relationship was not put asunder. The state now looked to the church to nurture the kind of Christians who would make good citizens. Mere morality would never produce "political prosperity." Religion was the taproot of the tree of liberty, as George Washington made clear in his Farewell Address: "Of all the dispositions and habits which lead to political prosperity, religion and morality are indispensable supports. In vain would that man claim the tribute of patriotism who should labor to subvert these great pillars of human happiness . . . and let us with caution indulge the supposition that morality can be maintained without religion."[1]

Surprising as it may sound in our secular age, the much misconstrued phrase "separation of church and state" cannot be found in the United States Constitution or in the Bill of Rights. The First Amendment religious clause simply states "Congress shall make no law respecting an establishment of religion, or prohibiting the free exercise thereof."

Thomas Jefferson, revered as the architect of the famous "wall of separation between church and state," was in France when Congress adopted the First Amendment, which James Madison wrote. Jefferson's reference to a "wall of separation between church and state" is the last phrase of a laborious sentence in a letter he sent to an association of Baptists in Danbury, Connecticut, in 1802, when he was President of the United States:

> Believing with you that religion is a matter which lies solely between man and his God, that he owes account to none other for his faith or his worship, that the legislative powers of government reach actions only, and not opinion, I contemplate with solemn reverence that act of the whole American People which declared that their legislature should "make no law

respecting an establishment of religion, or prohibiting the free exercise thereof," thus building a wall of separation between church and state.[2]

With those words Jefferson was not formulating a secular principle to banish religion from the public arena. Rather he was trying to keep government from darkening the doors of church. Neither Baptists nor the Deist Jefferson ever entertained the thought that religion was a divisive element in American society, which should be shoved onto the sidelines, to be mentioned only in church on Sunday. Yet absolutists in matters of church-state separation continually cite Jefferson's "wall" metaphor.

One could argue that it is doubtful Jefferson would have wanted a dangling phrase in a letter to become the cornerstone of a public policy decision. He opposed a religious monopoly but favored a free religious market where each sect could prosper as far as the persuasive powers of its preachers would carry it. In his pithy booklet, *Religion and the Constitution: A Reinterpretation*, Peter J. Ferrara states, "Jefferson's own conception of the wall of separation between church and state did not prevent him from advocating and implementing government for religious education in the state of Virginia."[3]

History shows that we are an incurably religious nation. Recent polls state that 95 to 99 percent of the people in this country believe in God. Experience teaches us that our religious convictions inform our political principles. We may separate the institutions of church and state, but we will never be able to separate politics and religion.

Nor should we ever try.

Puritan preachers were the first to formulate a "theology of liberation" to convince colonists that resistance against the British was biblically justified. Church and state marched in lockstep during the Revolutionary War to achieve their two-fold goal: to throw off the political yoke of Mother England and to prevent the establishment of the Anglican Church in the colonies.

The American Revolution was seen as a holy war. It was far from that, of course, but that was the popular perception. This righteous rebellion began in the churches before spilling out into the streets of Boston and the rural regions of the colonies. In 1776 mixing politics and religion was as common as drinking smuggled tea.

The religious side of American history has suffered from a seeming conspiracy of silence between authors of textbooks and teachers. Students continue to graduate from high school and college blissfully bereft of any knowledge of the pivotal part religion played in the American Revolution in the formation of our present political beliefs.

To require religion to stand mute in any public debate deprives the nation of a voice that needs to be heard. We dare not muzzle morality in the marketplace or permit the wall of separation to turn into an Iron Curtain of religious repression. Religion has always been a vital force in this country and never more so than at the beginning. The colonial clergy created the religious climate that made it possible for the American Revolution to take place. If that premise is true, then surely we can find a role for religion to play in the public arena in the twentieth century. We must never overlook our religious roots.

All Americans, old as well as young, need to recapture the religious essence of our national history. Our past, too precious to ignore, contains lessons that will help us deal with the present and that will spiritually undergird us to face the future.

YANKEE DOODLE
WENT *to* CHURCH

ONE

"Oh, Glorious Morning!"

1:00 A.M., April 19, 1775.

The square-jawed silversmith from Boston dismounted surprisingly quickly for a man his size, muscled his way past an indignant sergeant of the guard who tried blocking his path, and pounded on the front door of the Lexington parsonage.

"Come in, Paul Revere," John Hancock shouted. "We are not afraid of you."

Revere pushed open the door and strode into the dimly lit room, to be warmly greeted by the Reverend Jonas Clarke, pastor of the First Parish Church (Congregational) in Lexington, and his two guests, John Hancock and Sam Adams.

Revere informed the trio that seven hundred British troops—the elite grenadiers and light infantry—were on their way to Lexington and Concord. This messenger said the prime mission of the troops was to seize the military supplies at Concord. But it was also feared that the troops might try to arrest Hancock and Adams. Bagging the leading revolutionaries of rebellious Boston would be quite a coup.

Having delivered the warning, Revere ran back out into the night and mounted his horse to continue his ride into American history books—and into the arms of several British officers on the road to Concord. Revere was captured but eventually released. (Another rider would have to spread the alarm to the Concord militia.)

Hancock, Adams, and Clarke held a quick council of war. Should they call out the Lexington militia? Was this the time and place to start the shooting? Would the Lexington militia fire on the best-trained troops on the face of the globe—the king's own?

Clarke reassured his skeptical guests that the men of Lexington—though simple farmers, mill hands, and mechanics—were brave and as willing to fight as any Boston patriot. As most of the militiamen were members of his own church, Clarke had seen to it that Sunday after Sunday they were exposed to the kind of patriotic preaching guaranteed to produce "Christian soldiers."

Clarke's congregation "was ripe for revolution," the historian J. T. Headley wrote ninety years later, "ready to fight and to die rather than yield to arbitrary force." Calling Clarke "one of the most uncompromising patriots of the day," the writer asserted: "Earnestly, yet without passion, he discussed from the pulpit the great questions at issue, and that powerful voice thundered forth the principles of personal, civil and religious liberty, and the right of resistance, in tones as earnest as it had the doctrine of salvation by the cross."[1]

Hancock and Adams liked what they heard—even though they fully recognized that firing on the British regulars would be no Boston tea party. It was an act of war.

Hancock was chairman of the Committee of Safety, which had been invested with broad powers by the Provincial

Congress. The committee had the authority to call out the entire Massachusetts militia, under certain conditions.

The Congress had directed that whenever troops "to the Number of Five Hundred shall march out of Boston . . . it ought to be deemed a design to carry into execution by Force the late Acts of Parliament . . . and therefore the Military Forces of the Province ought to be assembled and an Army of Observation immediately formed, to *act solely on the defensive* so long as it can be justified on the principles of Reason and Self-Preservation and *no longer.*"[2]

The directive was flexible enough to accommodate a multitude of interpretations. How do you define "reason," and where does a "defensive" act become blurred with an offensive action?

Actually, Hancock, Adams, and Clarke may not have spent a great deal of time discussing finer points of the wording of the congressional directive. All three seemed to be spoiling for a fight.

Hancock was a minuteman at heart, who was convinced his military talents were never fully appreciated by his fellow colonists. Later he would feel deeply hurt when the Continental Congress bypassed him and named George Washington commander in chief of the American army.

Adams recognized that his forte was firing verbal volleys at the English Parliament rather than taking potshots at British Redcoats. But that didn't prevent him from providing opportunities for younger and more able-bodied men to prove their military mettle on the battlefield.

The bravery of the Reverend Jonas Clarke was beyond question. If there had to be a shooting war, he was willing for it to start on his own church green.

Thus a merchant-smuggler, a patriot-propagandist, and a Puritan preacher (Clarke), talking in a dark, quiet parsonage, agreed to the calling out of the militia—and by so doing helped trigger the American Revolution.

At 2:00 A.M., the bell atop the barnlike meetinghouse broke the early morning quiet. The same clanging that called the people of Lexington to worship now called the men of the village to do combat with the world's biggest and best army.

When the militia assembled, the Reverend Clarke was the first man to greet them. The commander of both the militia and alarm companies, Captain John Parker, forty-five, was a veteran of the French and Indian War. Parker knew that the British troops were intent on destroying the military stores in Concord. He saw his assignment as that of protecting the town only if the British attacked first.

The men waited for about an hour, then decided Revere had been wrong. The British apparently would not come after all. Parker ordered his men to disband but to stay on the alert. A few went back to the homes bordering on the village commons. Most spent the remainder of the early morning in Buckman's Tavern.

Suddenly, the shooting of the alarm guns, the insistent clanging of the church bell, and the beat of the drums broke the morning stillness. In the early light of dawn on an unseasonably warm morning, the men of Lexington once again scampered toward the village green. The scarlet and white colors of the British regulars were now visible as their troops marched silently down the curving hill that leads into Lexington.

Sergeant William Munroe was commanded by Parker to assemble the men in two ranks "a few rods [30 to 50 feet] northerly of the meeting house."[3]

At this point, Sam Adams, his lips twitching and trembling perhaps more than usual (he had the palsy), walked over to John Hancock, put his hand on his shoulder, and said, "This is not our business, John. We belong to the cabinet." A reluctant Hancock put down his weapon, and the two revolutionaries left the parsonage a short time before the British troops marched into Lexington.

As the militia—about forty in all—stood waiting, Captain Parker, even more impressed by the number of British troops as they came closer, ordered: "Let the troops pass by, and don't molest them, without they begin first."

British Marine Major John Pitcairn (who was Paul Revere's neighbor in Boston) also wanted to avoid bloodshed. Obviously the American militiamen were no match for his soldiers. He gave strict orders for his men not to fire "nor even attempt it, without orders."

Captain Parker, sizing up the odds, decided it unwise even to have an eyeball-to-eyeball confrontation with the British troops, and ordered his men to disperse.

But in the noise and confusion a nervous finger squeezed a trigger. No one knows whether it was British or American. Other shots were fired. Then there came a volley from the first platoon of British troops.

The shooting lasted only a few minutes. But when it was over, eight Americans lay dead or dying in front of the meetinghouse. Jonas Parker, the strongest wrestler in Lexington, who had sworn that morning he would never run from British soldiers, was killed, pierced by both ball and bayonet. Caleb Harrington died on the doorstep of the church, where he had run for powder.

The British had few casualties to report. Major Pitcairn's horse had been nicked, and one soldier was slightly wounded.

Adams and Hancock stopped when they heard the shots being fired. They were almost two miles away when the firing started. But to Adams the roar of the guns was the sound of music. He knew now there could be no turning back.

"Oh, what a glorious morning this is," Adams exclaimed.[4]
The American Revolution had begun.

The British troops, getting their first taste of American blood in a shoot-out, left shouting and in high spirits. They pushed their way on to Concord—where they would be rebuffed and sent reeling back to Boston in disarray and defeat.

The battle at Concord has received far more attention from historians than did the skirmish at Lexington. But the fact is, contrary to Emerson's immortal phrase, the first shots heard around the world were fired on a church green in Lexington— not on a rude bridge in Concord.

Figuratively the patriotic preaching of the Reverend Jonas Clarke primed those guns.

The Reverend William Ware of Cambridge wrote: "It would not be beyond the truth to assert that there was no person at that time and in that vicinity—not only no clergyman (but no other person of whatever calling or profession) who took a firmer stand for the liberties of the country, or was more ready to perform the duties and endure the sacrifices of a patriot, than the minister of Lexington."[5]

The Reverend Jonas Clarke, Puritan, preacher, patriot and propagandist, was a typical colonial clergyman. A graduate of Harvard (class of fifty-two), he was an articulate, intelligent, and moving force in the pulpit and in the public forum.

When only three years out of Harvard, Clarke was called to the First Parish Church, of Lexington, and given a lifelong tenure. He had preached in the Lexington pulpit for twenty years when the shots rang out on the green.

Clarke's wife and John Hancock were cousins, and the Boston war hawk was a frequent visitor in the Lexington parsonage. The two obviously were of one mind when it came to berating the British and baptizing the Whig cause. Clarke's sermon titles were giveaways as to which side God was on. On the first anniversary of the battle of Lexington, Clarke preached on the subject "The Fate of Blood Thirsty Oppressors and God's Tender Care of His Distressed People."

In a powerful voice that could be heard far outside the walls of the church, he thundered: "The Lord is a God that loveth righteousness and hateth iniquity, in whatever shape or character it appears. Injustice, oppression and violence (much less shedding of innocent blood) shall not pass unnoticed by the Governor of the world. Sooner or later a just recompense will be made upon such workers of iniquity."[6]

The Puritan pastor placed the blame for causing the colonies to revolt on British shoulders. "There is no just ground to suppose that *it would have ever entered the heart of Americans* to have desired a dissolution of so happy a connection with the mother country or to have sought independence of Britain, had they not been urged and even forced upon such an expedient by measures of oppression and violence and the shedding of innocent blood."[7]

Clarke hewed strictly to the Whig party line that the British had unconscionably violated the "chartered rights" of the colonies. The British Acts—the Stamp Act, Coercive Acts, and Mutiny Act—were more than infringements of colonists' civil rights—they were unrighteous as well. Moreover, the morally bankrupt British had the gall to send troops to America to enforce the illegal and ungodly acts of Parliament and "an innocent, loyal people are distressed."

The minister's eloquence and indignation rose to a crescendo in the conclusion of his anniversary sermon. Pastor Clarke fanned the flames of war from his vantage point in the pulpit. His account of the Lexington skirmish is revealing, albeit slanted:

At length on the night of 18th of April, 1775, the alarm is given of the hostile design of the [British] troops. Under cover of the darkness a brigade of these instruments of violence and tyranny make their approach, and with a quick and silent march on the morning of the 19th they enter this town. And this is the place where the fatal scene begins.

But O my God! How Shall I Speak! Or how describe the distress, the horror of that awful morn, that gloomy day! Yonder field can witness the innocent blood of our brethren slain. There the tender father bled, and there the beloved son. There the hoary head, and there the blooming youth![8]

Like many of his contemporaries, Clarke was a preacher-politician. John Hancock and Sam Adams often took advantage of his hospitality, spending time in his home to break bread and talk revolution. Clarke, a skilled theorist in government, had his advice and consent sought by the leading political figures throughout the Revolutionary period.

"For years before the Stamp Act," Alice M. Baldwin states in her definitive work, "he is said to have preached Sunday after Sunday and explained in many a town meeting the doctrines of natural and constitutional rights and the rights of resistance. He is said to have written practically every public paper of the town from 1762 to the end of the Revolutionary War, and every instruction to the Lexington delegates to the General Court [highest legislative body], some of which in his handwriting still remain."[9]

The Congregational minister had a way with words, and he was not hesitant to overstate a position, if he thought it would serve his purpose. Thus his attack on the Stamp Act: "We have looked upon men as being naturally free. What of all most alarms us is an Act commonly called the Stamp Act, the full execution of which we apprehend would divert us of our most inestimable charter rights and privileges, rob us of our character as free and natural subjects and of almost everything we ought as a people to hold dear."[10]

This minister, "who held his people in the hollow of his hand and who was friend and counsellor of statesmen,"[11] helped to shape the political contours of this nation. His powerful preaching and political theorizing were accepted as gospel truth by his enraptured listeners. He outlined "precept upon precept and line upon line" the right of free men to resist tyranny, even in its embryonic stage, and to alter and change their government to conform to their own mode. He was elected in 1779 to serve as representative to the constitutional convention.

In his Massachusetts Election Sermon of 1781, Clarke proclaimed that no one man or any number of men have a natural right or inherent claim to lord it over any men. "All men are by nature free and equal and independent in this matter," he said, echoing John Locke's natural law theory. "It is in compact, and in compact alone, that all government is founded."[12] Just as Congregationalists entered into a covenant with God and their brethren in the faith to form a church, so in the civil realm, men entered into a form of government of their own choosing by "compact." The limits of rulers as well as the responsibilities of the ruled were spelled out in that compact.

The right of men to select their own form of government is so sacred that even God abides by this principle, Clarke reasoned. Did not the Supreme Ruler, when establishing the "theocracy of the Hebrews," seek the "common consent" of the people before they covenanted with Him to live under His Law?

The appeal to Scripture to fortify a political position was common among Puritan preachers. When the showdown came with the British, the colonists had been properly conditioned to take up arms and resist, and few people fight as fiercely as those who believe they are engaged in a holy war. The majority of Americans perceived their Revolution as a righteous rebellion. In the minds of this eighteenth-century people, religious and civil freedom were intertwined. Losing one meant losing the other. A rent in the political fabric, even a small rip, could eventually lead to the unraveling of all those religious and political rights their Puritan forefathers had won on the battlefields, under Cromwell. Their ancestors had left their comfortable homeland for the hallowed "errand into the wilderness" in order to freely exercise those rights.

In the 1770s, in the minds of the majority the issue was a simple one: Colonists' rights were being eroded by the continual encroachment of an unrepresentative government, located 3,000 miles away, in London. They must nip tyranny in the bud, not permit it to grow to full bloom. Already British regulars had set foot on American soil, attempting to enforce illegal laws. Christian patriots had the solemn duty to resist. Failure to do so in such a just cause would bring them under God's condemnation.

Edmund Burke, who often served as interpreter of the colonists' cause in the British House of Commons, noted in 1775 that the Americans "augur misgovernment at a distance and snuff the approaching of tyranny in every tainted breeze."[13] Some of the loudest sniffing took place in Puritan pulpits.

The patriotic clergy—the hated Anglicans, the Quakers, and some Methodists opposed the rebellion for various reasons—provided the biblical justification essential to the Puritan laity, who would never have gone into battle had they not believed God was on their side. But if God became a Whig on Sunday, often His ways were replaced by the devil's methods during the week. Mobs roamed the streets, looting, trashing, stoning, and applying generous layers of tar and feathers (which burned the skin when applied and peeled the hide when removed) to unfortunate Tories.

Looking back on the fury of the American Revolution, both Whigs and Tories often were at a loss to explain its causes. "There was none of the legendary tyranny of history that had so often driven desperate people into rebellion," wrote the author of *Creation of the American Republic.* "The Americans were not an oppressed people; they had no crushing imperial shackles to throw off. In fact, the Americans knew they were probably freer and less burdened with cumbersome feudal and hierarchial restraints than any part of mankind in the eighteenth century."[14]

Why then the violence?

John Wingate Thornton, writing eighty-five years after the end of the Revolutionary War, felt convinced the clergy deserved a major share of the credit for fanning the flames of the Revolution, which burned America's political bridges with the British. "To the pulpit," Thornton thundered, "the *Puritan pulpit,* we owe the moral force which won our independence."[15]

Thornton's assessment of the influence of the clergy and the role of religion in the Revolution has been filtered out of most school textbooks on American history. The Revolution usually is described in terms of dates, battles, the Boston Tea Party, and protests against taxes. But focusing on the political and economic reasons for the Revolution, to the exclusion of the religious forces at work, distorts history.

No other class of people in colonial America could command the kind of hearing given the Puritan preacher every Sunday— sometimes twice on Sunday. The pulpit served as the platform from which the minister could mold the minds of the masses on a systematic, weekly basis. The minister spoke with divine authority—a right the colonists would deny mere kings—and the people listened, convinced they were hearing an oracle of God.

Colonial clergy couched political principles in biblical terms, developing their own "liberation theology." "Freedom in Christ" could easily be construed to mean political freedom as well as spiritual freedom. The militant war hawks of '76 were not interested in class struggle. They were content with the prevailing social arrangement. Their goal was to achieve self-government by cutting the political umbilical cord tying them to Mother England.

The Christian "ministers of war" had done their job well, infusing their congregants with the feeling they were first and foremost Christian soldiers marching as to war. Colonials had considered themselves people of the Book ever since the Pilgrims landed at Plymouth Rock. If God is for you, what does it matter that you are going out to do battle with the world's strongest army? God had always intervened in behalf of His Chosen People when they faced impossible odds. Equipped with the shield of faith and the sword of the Spirit, the poorly armed, ragtag American recruits set forth to do battle in the name of Jehovah God and the Continental Congress. In the process they would turn the world upside down.

TWO

The Molder of Minds

The Puritan divine, admired and respected, even if not always loved by his parishioners, stood tall in the pulpit, carefully choosing his words to "color the interior workings of the minds" of his congregation. He was aware he preached to an astute audience. New England churchgoers tasted, tested, and even savored sermons. Some families moved to another community for the sole purpose of finding preaching more to their liking, and the New England auditor could be caustic in his criticism. "I would rather hear my dog bark than Mr. Billings preach," one connoisseur of sermons in the village of Windham, Connecticut, remarked.[1] The ungifted Puritan preacher was better off to stand mute than to try to muddle his way through a poorly prepared and sloppily delivered sermon.

New England Puritan preachers mastered both the spoken and written word. Rigidly logical sermon structure, developed into an art form in the seventeenth century, was still in use a hundred years later. Colonial clergymen thought and spoke in concepts and biblical language familiar to the congregants, and certain biblical presuppositions undergirded early New England colonies.

The Puritan preacher gave logical, solid, scriptural—and often informative—sermons. Usually he laced his orations with current events. He often had the satisfaction of "flashing" the latest news bulletin, informing his congregation of the outcome of a battle or the death of a king and then interpreting its significance.

Brevity was not the colonial minister's long suit. He could preach for two hours, if necessary—and he often did. Normally he preached twice on Sundays—in the morning and in the afternoon. His sermons usually contained literary allusions to the Greek and Roman classics and quotations from the political writings of John Locke, Algernon Sidney, and John Milton—all encased, of course, within a biblical context.

Parsons ranked at the top of the social pecking order. "You must expect if you come to Danbury to be a good deal noticed or perhaps gazed at," wrote young Ebenezer Baldwin in 1763 to his sister, Bethiah, "for to be the minister's sister in a country town is a considerable thing."[2]

Clergymen were treated with the kind of reverential regard that Americans refused to give kings and Anglican bishops. Nineteenth-century writer William B. Sprague describes the almost electrifying effect the entrance of the minister and his family into the meetinghouse had on the congregation:

> The whole space before the meeting-house was filled with a waiting, respectful, and expecting multitude. At the moment of the service, the pastor issued from his mansion with Bible and manuscript sermon under his arm, with his wife leaning on one arm, flanked by a negro man on his side, as his wife was by her negro woman, the little negroes being distributed, according to their sex, by the side of their respective parents. Then followed every other member of the family, according to age and rank, making often, with family visitants, somewhat of a formidable procession.

As soon as it appeared, the congregation, as if moved by one spirit, began to move towards the door of the church; and, before the procession reached it, all were in their places. As soon as the pastor entered the church the whole congregation rose, and stood until the pastor was in the pulpit and his family were seated—until which was done, the whole assembly continued standing. At the close of the service, the congregation stood until he and his family had left the church, before any one moved toward the door. Forenoon and afternoon the same course of proceeding was had, expressive of the reverential relation in which the people acknowledged that they stood toward their clergyman.[3]

The argument is sometimes made that because only a small percentage of persons actually belonged to any church during the Revolutionary era, religion could not have been a vital factor. While the census bureau was not yet in existence, some historians estimate that as the Revolution approached, no more than one in eight persons belonged to a church in New England, and in the Middle Colonies and in the South the percentage was even smaller—one in fifteen and one in twenty, respectively.

After citing the above statistics, Arthur M. Schlesinger cautions: "It does not follow, however, that the rest were unbelievers. Some of them, in isolated regions, would have had to travel many miles to partake in public worship. Others considered they could lead upright lives without formal affiliation. Others had never undergone the emotional religious experience that was still demanded as a qualification for church membership."[4]

No matter how many people belonged to the church, Schlesinger makes the point "in the early days the pastor, especially in New England, had been the leading member of the community. He was not only the spiritual guide, on intimate terms with the Lord, but also the most learned person; and on both scores he was considered an unfailing fount of wisdom on public and private matters."[5]

Schlesinger recounts the revealing anecdote of a visitor who came to Andover, Massachusetts, and "asked Congregational minister Samuel Phillips whether he was 'the parson who serves here,' " Phillips tartly replied, " 'I am, Sir, the parson who rules here.' "[6]

James Truslow Adams argues that "by the opening of the new century [eighteenth], however, the power and the influence of the clergy were visibly declining. . . ."[7] Schlesinger agrees that "the passage of time wrought changes in the minister's position as business and other secular interests absorbed the increasing attention of the people and even some members of the cloth."[8]

Both men, however, are speaking in relative terms— comparing the influence of the eighteenth-century minister with that of his seventeenth-century counterpart. Obviously, the clergy exerted more control over the populace at the time of the settling of the New England colonies than they did in the latter part of the eighteenth century. Though his power may have diminished by the eighteenth century, the preacher still held a preeminent role in a basically religious society. Sydney Ahlstrom concludes that "Puritanism provided the moral and religious background of fully 75 percent of the people who declared their independence in 1776."[9] (The population of the thirteen colonies was approximately 2.5 million.)

A prominent colonial scholar, Patricia U. Bonomi, of New York University, challenges the view held by many historians that the clout of the clergy was considerably diminished at the turn of the eighteenth century. "For so many years," she wrote in her detailed study, *Under the Cope of Heaven: Religion, Society, and Politics in Colonial America,* "church historians asserted that no more than 5 to 20 percent of colonial Americans were churchgoers, and though that figure was based on little but rough impressions it has gained a wide circulation.

"Recent estimates, on the other hand," she states, "based on ministers' reports and on the ratio of congregations to inhabitants, indicate that no less than some 60 percent of the adult white population attended church regularly between 1700 and 1776."[10]

Professor Bonomi flatly disputes the widely held belief that Enlightenment ideas influenced political thought to a greater degree than did Puritan political principles. "An eighteenth century of 'Enlightenment' skepticism between a 'Puritan' seventeenth century and an 'evangelical' nineteenth century simply does not add up," she wrote. "Indeed it has recently been suggested that although the Enlightenment facilitated a range of responses to religious belief, atheism cannot be seen as one of them, and the latest community studies leave little doubt as to the vigor of religion in eighteenth-century American culture."[11]

Professor Bonomi's conclusions are supported by the oft-quoted on-the-scene observer from France, Alexis de Tocqueville, who wrote in the 1830s: "America is still the place where the Christian religion has kept the greatest influence over men's souls."[12]

The weight of scholarship is on the side of those who contend that as late as the eighteenth century Americans still took their religion seriously. Carl Bridenbaugh, a scholar of the colonial period and a history professor at Brown University, argues convincingly that we will never understand the mind of the eighteenth-century American if we "unconsciously omit, or consciously jam out, the religious theme just because our own milieu is secular."[13]

Bridenbaugh said our colonial forefathers "considered piety, religious observance, even theology, as part of their daily existence." He goes even farther to argue that the American Revolution took place in a "religious atmosphere." "It is indeed high time we repossess the important historical truth that religion was a fundamental cause of the American Revolution," he concludes.[14]

Colonial Americans continually argued politics and religion. They seldom separated the two, in the hinterlands as well as in the more sophisticated seaboard towns. A British official returning from a visit to rural Connecticut came back with the impression that "they are all politicians and they are all Scripture learnt."[15]

Students of the role religion played in the struggle for independence are compelled to consult Alice M. Baldwin's standard text, *The New England Clergy and the American Revolution*. Throughout her book, she continually emphasizes the part the pastor played in teaching political theory "to the people both before and after 1763." By merely mouthing political theories, the minister gave them the added appeal of having been sanctified.

Baldwin laments that "the intimate relation of the New England minister to the thought and life of eighteenth century New England has never been adequately developed." She corrected that oversight by delineating the "similarity, the identity of Puritan theology and fundamental political thought." She also demonstrated, through solid research, how "the New England clergy preserved, extended, and popularized the essential doctrines of political philosophy, thus making familiar to every church-going New Englander long before 1763 not only the doctrines of natural rights, the social contract, and the right of resistance but also the fundamental principle of American constitutional law, that government, like its citizens is bound by law and when it transcends its authority, it acts illegally."[16] For such principles the colonists fought—or at least so they thought.

The eighteenth-century spiritual leader was a many-sided man, educated and sophisticated as well as pious. He lived, moved, and had his being among the people he served. He was the most widely read and traveled of his contemporaries. Exposed to the latest religious and political thinking at colleges such as Harvard and Yale, he sat in town meetings and discussed the laws of nature and the God who ordained them, the biblical basis for government by compact, and the right to resist tyranny before it fastened the chains on the body politic. The ideas and views of the Puritan divine were sought by public officials, and those in the pews, who included the community's leading citizens as well as the lower classes—farmers, laborers, and mechanics—heeded his counsel. Puritan preachers did not confine their persuasive powers to the pulpit. They recognized the potency of the press and were fully aware that what they wrote would be widely read. By 1761, the Reverend Andrew Eliot could accurately state that "scarce any are to be found among us, even in the obscurest parts, who are not able to read and write with some tolerable propriety."[17]

By 1776, thirty-two journals were published, mostly in the principal seaports and provincial capitals, but they circulated throughout the countryside. The *Boston News Letter* had 500 to 600 subscribers and many more readers. Carl Bridenbaugh reveals that "north of Maryland in 1760, the printers of seven communities published fourteen weekly gazettes." He further states that between 1766 and 1768, twenty newspapers came out weekly in eleven places, and twenty-nine newspapers were published in fifteen New England towns, when the shots were first fired at Lexington. "Boston, New York, and

Philadelphia newspapers had an average circulation of 1,475 in 1765, which rose to 2,530 by 1774; those in smaller places ranged from 700 to 800 each."[18]

The clergy contributed political essays on the origin and end of government and flooded the press with warnings against the subtle encroachment of colonial rights by an unrepresentative Parliament, 3,000 miles away, in London.

The ministers adroitly dipped their goose quills in acid and composed stinging sentences to chastise their adversaries. Some of the running feuds between Whig and Tory preachers bordered on personal vendettas rather than dispassionate arguments on political issues. Christian charity seldom found its way into the newspaper columns.

The spoken word, however, remained the primary medium of shaping public opinion. In taverns, town meetings, and in church, colonial Americans discussed political and religious issues without bothering to separate the two.

"But it should be noted," Bridenbaugh wrote, "that though the Yankee picked up his practical politics in the local forum, he very likely got his political theory in ecclesiastical form from the minister on the Sabbath or at the weekly lecture. . . . For eighty-five years prior to the revolt of the colonies the Congregational divines used their pulpits to instill in the minds of a highly intelligent and interested townsfolk the connection between the law of God and the law of nature. . . ."[19]

Every year a minister was carefully selected by the politicians to deliver an election sermon on the last Wednesday in May at the time of the election of the general court—the upper house of the colonial legislature. This tradition dates back to 1633 in Massachusetts.

The election sermon guaranteed the preacher a public platform. As the shadow of the Revolution lengthened over the land, the patriots made sure that only "lovers of liberty" were nominated to preach the election sermon. Passages of sermons filled with patriotic phrases and Whig propaganda were "circulated far and wide by means of newspapers, and read with avidity and a degree of veneration on account of the preacher and his election to the service of the day," a contemporary historian assures us.[20]

The election sermons had their ripple effects in the countryside. They set the theme—and even the tone—of sermons that would be preached throughout the year in small village pulpits. The sermons became "textbooks in politics." And they were designed more to make good minutemen than to make men good. The sermons were studied, reworked, and then repeated so that the New Englander became "enlightened in speculative and practical politics to a degree unknown anywhere else in the world."[21]

Preachers also pressed their political views on the populace in sermons given on the day of the election of the militia officers, the annual spring fast, fall Thanksgiving day, and other special occasions. Patriotic ministers became experts at spontaneously formulating "liberty prayers." These pious, pithy appeals for the blessings of Providence on the patriot cause became a standard preface to political meetings.

Southern patriots also found prayer and fasting good politics. Thomas Jefferson, Patrick Henry, and Richard Henry Lee used the clergy in Virginia in 1774 to whip up patriotic emotions of those they feared were becoming cold in their love of liberty. The trio came to the conclusion that "the appointment of a day of general fasting and prayer would be most likely to call up and alarm their attention."[22]

The House of Burgesses approved the request, setting June 1, 1774, as the date. Each member of the house sent a copy of the resolution to the clergymen in his county. The plan produced the expected results.

"The people met generally," Jefferson recorded, "with anxiety and alarm in their countenances, and the effect of the day thro' the whole colony was like a shock of electricity, arousing every man and placing him on his centre."[23] Jefferson may have been a Deist who liked to scissor the Scriptures to fit his own peculiar, tailor-made religion, but he recognized that in eighteenth-century America, the most effective way to mold public opinion was by making common cause with the clergy.

No one knew better than the Tories that the clergy constituted a formidable foe. Daniel Leonard, a Tory pamphleteer who wrote under the pseudonym of "Massachusettensis," warned:

> When the clergy engage in political warfare, religion becomes a most powerful engine, either to support or to overthrow the state. What effect it must have had upon the audience, to hear the same sentiments and principles, which they had read before in a newspaper, delivered on Sundays from the sacred desk with religious awe, and the most solemn appeals to Heaven, from lips, which they had been taught from their cradles, to believe could utter nothing but eternal truths.[24]

Leonard was not alone in his criticism of clergy who turned their pulpits into propaganda platforms to further the Whig cause. Freedom of speech, on the eve of the Revolution, had been practically abrogated by mob rule in Boston. Declaring one's allegiance to the "powers that be" (namely, King George III), as Scripture commands, could result in a "loyalist robe" of tar and feathers. The loyalist could find no comfort in the church—unless he attended an Episcopal house of worship.

Peter Oliver, a wealthy loyalist who served as Chief Justice of Massachusetts before his property was appropriated and he fled to England for safety, would contemptuously refer to "Mr. [James] Otis's black regiment, the dissenting clergy, who took so active part in the Rebellion."

"The town of Boston being the Metropolis," Oliver wrote, "it was also the Metropolis of Sedition; and hence it was that their Clergy being dependent on the People for their daily Bread; by having frequent Intercourse with the People, imbibed their principles."[25]

Jonathan Sewall, a Harvard classmate and fellow lawyer of John Adams, soon found himself outside the political pale because of his loyalist leanings. Sewall's ardent support of the crown had had its earthly rewards—he had been appointed solicitor general, advocate general, and attorney general of Massachusetts. But before the war was over, Sewall had been cast out of his own country, stripped of his property and pride. A broken figure, he would never again see the land he loved. He died brokenhearted and still bewildered by the events that hit the colonies with the force of a hurricane. Sewall castigated the clergy for their role in the Revolution: "The simple, unmeaning mechanic, peasant, and laborer, who had really no Interest in the Matters of the Controversy, hood-wink'd, inflamed and goaded by their *spiritual drivers*, fancied they saw civil and religious tyranny advancing with hasty strides; and thus the Flames soon spread thro these provinces, and by the help of Kindred Spirits on the other side of the Atlantic it at length spread thro the continent."[26]

Whig and Tory alike agreed that the clergy played the pivotal role in fomenting the rebellion that eventually erupted into a revolution. The Puritan pulpit was the Whig's secret weapon. The clergy had produced the kind of mind-set in their parishioners that made them see political and religious issues as separate sides of the same coin.

"Thus the church polity of New England," Thornton wrote, "begat like principles in the state. The pew and the pulpit had been educated to self-government. They were accustomed 'to *consider*.' This highest glory of the American Revolution, said John Quincy Adams, was this: it connected in one indissoluble bond, the principle of civil government with the principles of Christianity."[27]

THREE

The Religious Roots of the American Revolution

The American Revolution was a transplant. Its roots, watered by the Atlantic Ocean, stretched all the way back to England's fertile soil, which gave growth to so many religious rivalries. The "swarming of the Puritans" to America because of religious persecution "simply put off for 150 years, and moved to another land"[1] the final struggle between the Royalists in church and state and the religious and civil Independents.

The Puritan roots might be said to lie with King Henry VIII. England's rupture with Rome took place when King Henry formed his own national church—probably more for political purposes than for religious reasons.[2] The new church remained Catholic in doctrine and worship—with certain minor modifications. But Henry still saw himself as the Defender of the Faith, a title given him by Pope Leo X.[3]

As if by divine decree, Martin Luther's launching of the Protestant Reformation in Germany and Gutenberg's invention of movable type came together in the same land and at the same time. The "stubborn monk" challenged the king of Kings—the pope—and won. In the Middle Ages the Bible had been a closed book to everyone except the learned and the rich. Now printing presses sprang up, and the Bible was translated into the vernacular. The Word of God, implanted in the hearts and minds of the peasants, would beget ideas of the rights of man that later would topple princes and powers.

Often people overlook the fact that England, in the words of historian Will Durant, had a rehearsal of the Reformation 130 years before it broke out in Germany. "All the major elements of the Reformation were in Wyclif," Durant states.[4] The first of the English Reformers led the revolt against the worldliness of the clergy, emphasized salvation by grace rather than by good works, and protested against the state subordinating itself to the papacy and the sending of national wealth to Rome. But Wyclif's most revolutionary contribution to Christianity was his belief that the Bible should be available to any Englishman who could read.

One hundred and thirty years later, King Henry VIII ordered every church to install a Bible written in English rather than the authorized Latin version. The consequences of that single act "have come thundering down through the centuries. For the first time, Englishmen could examine Holy Writ for themselves and come to their own conclusion about it, without the benefit of clergy."[5]

King Henry hardly could have conceived what he had wrought by making the Bible an open book in English society. He had, in effect, removed the heavy hand of the clergy and forced Englishmen to think for themselves and to act as their consciences dictated. History was being diverted into a new channel. This inalienable right to independence of judgment later would serve as the backbone for those stiff-necked American colonists who refused to bend to English demands.

King Henry's substitution of the Anglican Church for the Roman Catholic Church did not mean that all his subjects became devout Anglicans overnight. Most Englishmen sympathized with the Roman Catholic Church up to the time of the defeat of the Spanish Armada, in 1588.

The children of King Henry and his various wives changed the complexion of the national church to match their own personal religious views. Edward VI (1547–1553) "purified" the English Church of most of its Catholicism. Under Edward, clergy were permitted to marry, confession was abolished, the reading of Scripture was encouraged, and English replaced Latin in the worship services.

Edward was succeeded by Mary Tudor (1553–1558), the daughter of Henry and his first wife, Catherine of Aragon. Mary reversed the Edwardian reforms, reinstituted the Roman rite, and placed England in spiritual subjection to the pope.

"Mary," nicknamed *Bloody Mary*, who became England's most hated queen, "was by nature and habit merciful—til 1555," Durant notes.[6] Convinced that God was angry with her because she had been too lenient with heretics, she unleashed a reign of terror. The persecution that followed would be etched so deeply into the religious memories of English Dissenters that it would fuel the fires of bigotry for generations to come.

Queen Elizabeth succeeded her half sister, Mary. Once again the religious policy of the country was reversed. Elizabeth severed relations with Rome and outlawed Catholic Church rites. But she still had enough of the Catholic faithful in her realm to make her sensitive to their religious preferences and political clout.

In an attempt to appease all factions in her kingdom,

Queen Elizabeth served up a kind of religious stew that contained something for everybody—except for the hard-core Puritans, who were increasingly becoming a thorn in the side of her throne. "Despite Puritan protests, she maintained the Episcopal government, a creed which bore the imprint of Lutheranism, and a liturgy borrowed from Medieval Roman Catholicism."[7] The state's control of the national church displeased both the Catholic-minded Anglicans and the growing number of Puritans. "But the Anglican Church was Catholic enough to satisfy the moderate Catholics, and Protestant enough to satisfy the moderate Protestants, and combined they made up a large majority of the English People."[8]

During Queen Elizabeth's reign Puritanism developed into a potent religious force. Originally the Puritans had no intention of withdrawing from the Church of England, because they believed they could cleanse the church from within by changing its polity from prelacy to the Presbyterian form of government and by abolishing certain vestiges of Catholic rituals.

The Puritans seemed at times to major in minors. They opposed formalism in worship, wearing of clerical vestments, the making of the sign of the cross in baptism, and keeping holy days. They hungered to hear the Word of God preached to them in their own mother tongue.

The term *Puritan* gradually took on more political coloring, becoming identified with the left wing of the English Reformation. Queen Elizabeth became increasingly uneasy with the growing Puritan faction. Fearing a collision between the zealous Reformers and the Catholics in her kingdom could lead to civil war, she resorted to the trusted political gambit of playing one side off against the other.

The Puritans gradually turned their efforts from changing

church practices to reforming manners and morals. This upset Queen Elizabeth even more. But the stern Puritan morality produced positive results.

The more visible the Puritans became in England, the better targets they made. King James I, who followed Elizabeth on the English throne, zeroed in on the Dissenters with a royal vengeance. "I shall make them conform or I will harry them out of the land, or else do worse," he stormed at the Hampden Court conference in 1604.[9] The king's "peppering of the Puritans"—to use his own terminology—eventually boomeranged and, ironically, contributed to the downfall of his dynasty. His oppressive policies helped to transmute the Puritan religious movement into a political party. Many persons flocked to the Puritans' banner, not so much because they shared their religious beliefs, but because they wanted to help keep a power-hungry king in check.

King James was more of a prophet than he realized. He did indeed "harry" many a Puritan out of the land—most of them eventually emigrated to New England.

In the sixteenth century, radical religious reforms sprouted on the campus of Cambridge University and spread, infiltrating all strata of society. The Cambridge scholars and students mined Scripture and became convinced that the primitive Christian faith had been corrupted by time and "human invention." Their views upset the orthodox and earned them the epithet of "those precise men." The terms stuck. The Reformers were soon known all over England as the *Precisians*, a pejorative phrase later changed to *Puritan*.[10]

As the authority of Scripture increased, the power of the national church over local congregations diminished. Puritan-controlled churches boldly declared that their congregations existed by the authority of God rather than that of the national church. Thus "incipient Congregationalism" began seeping into the ecclesiastical corridors of the Church of England.

English Congregationalists still subscribed to the concept of a national church. But in their eyes the Church of England was a federation of autonomous churches rather than a monolithic structure with power wielded by bishops and peaking at the throne.

Puritan political philosophy called for the civil government to enforce church and civil laws. The magistrate was supposed to deal with heretics, for instance. But the state was not to meddle in the internal matters of local churches. This concept assumed close cooperation between church and state.

The Puritan construct of the ideal church-state relationship had one major flaw—King James wouldn't go along with it. No king was going to protect a church and enforce its laws while it harbored a growing number of religious radicals asserting the king had no authority over their religious lives. (Many Puritans, of course, leapfrogged that problem by sailing to America and setting up their own commonwealth.)

The Congregationalists, who held that the people in the congregation had power over it, split from the Puritan party and subsequently divided into two camps—Separatists and Nonseparatists.

The Separatists emphasized the primitive purity of the church. They argued that a true church consisted only of those persons who had been truly converted to Christ. This meant that the elect had to prove they had been elected to God by pointing to a precise time and place in which they had encountered God in Christ. After a group of Christians had validated their spiritual conversions, these "proved saints" entered into a covenant with themselves and with God to form a congregation. It was that simple—and that difficult.

It was obvious to the Separatists that many of the nonelect

were warming pews in the established Church of England. This left them with only one choice—to withdraw from the spiritually polluted church. Our Pilgrim Fathers did this.

The Nonseparatists were more flexible in the matter of fellowship. They agreed that only tried and true saints should be admitted to church membership and that each local church was its own authority. But they differed with the Separatists over whether the Church of England was a true church according to scriptural standards.

Nonseparatists believed a leaven of proven saints in the Anglican Church preserved a kernel of truth "in the husks of corruption." The Separatists and Nonseparatists theoretically agreed in church polity (Congregationalism), and both subscribed to the principle of compulsory uniformity in religion. But the Nonseparatists considered themselves loyal members of the Church of England.

The two factions also differed in their attitude toward the king. The Pilgrims, who were Separatists, recognized King James I as their sovereign and lord. Thus before landing at Plymouth Rock, the Pilgrims signed the Mayflower Compact, which began: "In the Name of God, Amen. We, whose names are underwritten, the Loyal Subjects of our dread Sovereign Lord King James, by the Grace of God, of Great Britain, France, and Ireland, King, Defender of the Faith, etc."

That same compact, which Samuel Eliot Morison calls, "an almost startling revelation of the capacity of Englishmen in that era for self-government,"[11] made it clear what the priorities of that hardy band were: "Having undertaken for the Glory of God, and the Advancement of the Christian Faith, and the Honour of our King and Country, a Voyage to plant the first colony in the northern Part of Virginia. . . ."

The Nonseparatist Puritans, on the other hand, embraced

the Church of England as their spiritual mother while holding the king at arm's length and seeking reformation in the church.

Eventually the Nonseparatists in New England like the Separatists, made the congregation the focus of all authority. The people ordained their own pastors and elected their own church officers. This pristine Congregational policy gradually changed, incorporating a kind of modified Presbyterianism. Power eventually became concentrated in the hands of the pastor, elders, and teachers and less in the pew itself. The Congregationalist Church became the established church in Massachusetts, Connecticut, and what is now New Hampshire.

Miter and scepter united during the reign of King Charles I to stifle Puritanism. The king commissioned William Laud, the beefy, red-faced Archbishop of Canterbury, to cleanse the Church of England and the body politic of the contagious Puritan infection. Laud carried out his assignment with holy zeal. He arrested Puritans and then pushed for swift justice in drumhead hearings before the courts, the secret Star Chamber, and the High Commission. Archbishop Laud's tactics paid off. Puritans fled to New England by the thousands, earning Laud the sarcastic title "father of New England."

The Puritans who formed the Massachusetts Bay Company were a rare breed of people. Their leader, John Winthrop, was a man of wealth who had attended Trinity College, Cambridge. And Winthrop was in the vanguard of what historians term the "swarming of the Puritans" to America.

Once the mass exodus began, it gathered speed and force, until it became a virtual torrent of ships packed with bodies and supplies. Seventeen ships, carrying 1,000 passengers, sailed from England to Massachusetts Bay in 1630. More than 20,000 colonists would migrate to America in that decade.

John Winthrop crossed in the flagship—the *Arbella*. Winthrop had in his possession a most precious document—the Charter of the Massachusetts Bay Colony. Instead of being controlled by a company based in England, as the Pilgrims were at the outset, from the start the Puritans who settled Massachusetts Bay, had freedom to govern themselves practically as they pleased.

Historian Charles M. Andrews observed that the Massachusetts Bay Colony "was led by the largest and most important group of men that ever at any time came over the seas to New England; men of wealth and education, of middle-class origin with a quantum of political training, hard-headed and dogmatic."[12]

In contrast, the Pilgrims were a mix—some poor and a few well-to-do. George F. Willison tells us that for the most part, the Pilgrims were "farmers and artisans. There was not a drop of blue blood on board that vessel [*Mayflower*] or any of the Pilgrim ships that followed."[13]

But whether rich or poor, those first immigrants merged into a nation unlike any other on the face of the earth. Protected by a "moat" 3,000 miles wide, isolated from the prevailing political and social trends that whipped across England and Europe, conditioned by a rugged, hostile environment, and motivated by a belief in a divine destiny, American colonists were by nature free, independent, self-sufficient—and downright cantankerous.

"The majority of those destined to people New England insisted upon going to heaven in their own way," Van Tyne wrote. "And from this chronic and incurable nonconformity in religion, developed political opposition to rulers who would drive them along the Episcopalian road to salvation."[14]

Van Tyne further states a theme that cannot be emphasized enough if we are to understand our national heritage. "The idea of the sovereignty of the people, the modern world's dominant ideal of democratic rule, may be said to have originated in the days of Elizabeth and James with those small congregations of Separatists who asserted their right to meet and worship in their own way."[15]

The despised sects of England flourished in the free air of the New World. They put their principles into motion as soon as they set foot on shore. The written compact was the hallmark of our nation's original settlers. As Sweet states, all those bedrock freedoms we cherish today—freedom of speech and of the press, freedom of conscience, freedom to worship, individual liberties—can be traced back to the beliefs of those religious radicals who populated New England.[16]

FOUR

Errand Into the Wilderness

Members of the Company of the Massachusetts Bay held a stockholders meeting in Southampton in March of 1630, shortly before an estimated seven hundred persons set sail for America in eleven ships. But instead of listening to a financial report, these "stockholders," ever mindful of God's call to His Chosen People, heard a sermon. The preacher, the gifted John Cotton, would not be making the journey. He took as his text 2 Samuel 7:10: "Moreover I will appoint a place for my people Israel, and will plant them, that they may dwell in a place of their own, and move no more. . . ." Cotton reminded the Puritan sojourners headed for a strange land that they were to live by the ordinances of God. "You shall never find," he assured his listeners, "that God ever rooted out a people that had the ordinances planted among them, and themselves planted into the ordinances. Never did God suffer such plants to be pulled up."[1]

The Massachusetts Bay Company was chartered by the crown in 1629, and John Winthrop was elected governor. In the same year, two Nonseparatist Puritan ministers, Francis Higginson and Samuel Skelton, were among an advance party that established a Congregational Church in Salem. Their congregation adopted a confession of faith and solemnly entered into a covenant relationship with God and with one another. Although both men had been ordained in the Church of England, the congregation ordained Skelton as pastor and Higginson as teacher. Thus the first Nonseparatist church with the congregational form of government was planted on the shores of America.

Winthrop took the Massachusetts Bay Colony charter with him when he boarded the *Arbella,* because this worldly-wise man was taking no chances. The Massachusetts Bay Colony was an open corporation. That left it vulnerable to be taken over by a block of unbelievers who could change the whole character of the company. Winthrop, determined to protect the purity of the company, kept the charter in his hip pocket.

On paper the Company of Massachusetts Bay was a business undertaking "to exploit the land, the sea and their resources. . . ." But the Puritans who controlled the company had other ideas.

In the middle of the voyage, John Winthrop "took the precaution to drive out of their heads any notion that in the wilderness the poor and the mean were ever to improve themselves as to mount above the rich or the eminent in dignity. Were there any who had signed up under the mistaken impression that such was the purpose of their errand, Winthrop told them that, although other peoples, lesser breeds, might come for wealth or pelf, this migration was specifically dedicated to an avowed end that had nothing to do with incomes."[2] Those aboard the *Arbella* and her sister ships had entered into a covenant with God to engage in a divine mission. If any turned aside and placed their affections on carnal pleasures or material gains, then the Jehovah God of the Covenant would break in upon them in His awesome wrath.

Winthrop's spiritual blueprint for the migration was contained in his lay sermon, "A Modell of Christian Charity." Winthrop described how the Puritans would know that God had agreed to enter into a covenant with them: "Now if the Lord shall please to hear us, and bring us in peace to the place we desire, then He has ratified this covenant and sealed our commission. . . ."[3]

But the covenant also contained a "strict performance" clause. To make the covenant binding, the immigrants would have "to do justly, to love mercy, to walk humbly with our God," as the prophet Micah had explained to a Chosen People of ancient times.

Winthrop dealt directly with matters of church and state. By "mutual consent," the English immigrants would live together under a "due form of Government both civil and ecclesiastical."[4] A due ecclesiastical government to Winthrop could mean only one thing: a form of church government patterned after New Testament principles. The label *Congregational* later would be given to it, but to Winthrop it "was no denominational peculiarity but the very essence of organized Christianity."[5]

Winthrop held equally rigid views on what constituted a due civil government: "A political regime, possessing power, which would consider its main function to be the erecting, protecting, and preserving this form of [Congregational] polity."[6] The civil government also would make sure that there was complete conformity in matters of worship and doctrine and that dissenters would be subdued, or banished.

Our spiritual forefathers would have been appalled at our political Founding Fathers who brought forth on this continent government of the people, for the people, and by the people. Democracy, Winthrop could assert, "has always been accounted the meanest and worst of all forms of government."[7] This country was not settled by those seeking religious freedom. They came here to worship as they pleased, and those who disagreed had the freedom to stay away.

Winthrop recognized, however, that the kind of church-state he envisioned could only work if lubricated by love. The true spirit of this unusual man is found in the following paragraph from his sermon, "A Modell of Christian Charity":

> For this end, we must be knit together in this work as one man. We must hold each other in brotherly affection; we must be willing to rid ourselves of our excesses to supply others' necessities; we must uphold a familiar commerce together in all meekness, gentleness, patience, and liberality. We must delight in each other, make others' conditions our own and rejoice together, mourn together, and suffer together . . . as members of the same body.[8]

It was a "model" never achieved in the rugged environment of wilderness America, but it was a lofty ideal worthy of the man who penned it.

Winthrop emphasized that the Puritans' "errand into the wilderness" was being closely watched and that nothing less than the honor of God was at stake. If they succeeded (by keeping the covenant and walking in the ordinances of God) then "men shall say of succeeding plantations [colonies], 'The Lord make it like that of New England.' For we must consider that we shall be like a City upon a Hill. The eyes of all the people are upon us."[9]

The first ships in the Puritan fleet arrived in Salem in

June—much better timing than the Pilgrims, who came ashore on a wintry November day. The original settlers at Salem, however, were not models of Christian charity. The "old planters" gave the newcomers a rather frosty reception. Winthrop's group eventually settled on a peninsula that they called Boston, after the town in Lincolnshire, England.

The Puritans who settled on the Massachusetts Bay during the years of the great migration set about establishing their "due forms" of church and political government. The Massachusetts Bay Company had a governor (president), vice-governor (vice-president), and a board of directors called the court of assistants. The freemen elected new members and annually chose officers of the company. The association met four times a year. These meetings were called sessions of the Great and General Court of Massachusetts.

As the population increased, it became increasingly difficult to get all the freemen together in one place. The first meeting of the general court in Boston was held October 19, 1630, the year Winthrop's fleet arrived. By 1632 there were at least eight newly created towns on or near Boston Bay. By 1634 the general court had developed into a representative assembly of several towns. Two years later, the general court was converted into a bicameral body, with the court of assistants becoming the upper house. (The court of assistants was dissolved in 1684, when the original charter was revoked. It was replaced by the governor's council.)

On May 18, 1631, the general court handed down the edict, "Noe man shall be admitted to the freedom of this body politicke, but such as are members of some of the churches within the limites of the same."[10]

The general court's ruling violated the charter, but the Puritans interpreted the charter to suit their own purposes. They intended to keep the government in the hands of "honest and good men." The Puritans were never impressed with majority rule. Israel never had a democracy, and Winthrop saw no need to establish one in America. As a result, the Bay Colony was under the "rulership of the redeemed" and those privileged church members who had been given the franchise. In 1643, thirteen years after the *Arbella* arrived, only 1,708 persons out of a total population of 15,000 in the Bay Colony were considered citizens with the right to vote and to participate in the political process.

Historians differ on their interpretation of the influence the clergy exerted in civil affairs in seventeenth-century New England. The Commonwealth of Massachusetts, however, was never a *theocracy*, if by that term one means "a state ruled by the clergy." Although the state enforced the laws of the church and protected its doctrinal purity, ministers were not permitted to hold public office.

The Puritan minister still had considerable clout. Congregationalism was the established church in Massachusetts. Only church members could vote. So the clergy determined who qualified for church membership. Thus when a minister examined a potential member of his congregation—making sure he had been converted and "elected" by God to salvation—he also screened a future citizen. The clergy derived political power by exercising their priestly function.

By 1645, Massachusetts had twenty-three churches to serve an estimated population of 15,000. Between 1630 and 1642, sixty-five ministers, most of whom were graduates of Cambridge University, arrived in Massachusetts.[11] From the beginning the clergy was the best educated and most influential class in colonial America. Ministers continued to exert a disproportionate amount of influence up to the time of the American Revolution. They lived among their people, acting as arbitrators in disputes and correcting those who showed signs of weakening in the faith. They were consulted as the final authority on Scripture, around which all areas of life revolved, and dispensed advice on a multitude of matters. Although in a technical sense, the Puritan community could not be defined as a theocracy, in a real sense it was. God was the Divine Monarch; the Bible was the living Word of God; and the clergy had been called of God to interpret His Word to the people of the covenant.

The covenant theory, sometimes called federal theology, began with an agreement between God and man. The regenerate man, usually referred to as a saint, promised to obey God's will, and God promised to grant him salvation. The concept of the divine partnership between God and a single saint was extended to the church and the state.

Authority in the church rested with the saints, who delegated it to their pastors, teachers, elders, and deacons—the officers of the church. Thus the church was a "speaking aristocracy in the face of a silent democracy."[12] (The unregenerate majority in the community could not participate in either church or civil affairs. However, they were required to attend worship services and pay taxes.)

The Puritans "argued that a nation of saints, all of whom were personally in covenant with God, would also be in covenant with Him as a body politic. . . ." Just as an individual could enter into a covenant with God, so could a corporate political body. As long as the "owners of the covenant" obeyed God's ordinances, He would reward their faithfulness. "Under these happy conditions, the New Englanders believed that their governments, alone among the nations of the earth, had been founded. . . ."[13]

Puritans believed the Bible was self-explanatory, as Sweet explained Scripture was compared with Scripture to arrive at the proper meaning. The Bible defined doctrine, polity, and government. Dissensions could be attributed only to a misin-terpretation or a misunderstanding of Scripture, because all Scripture had been plainly written that "he that runneth may read." Those who continued to dissent were visited by a minister, who attempted to put the erring brother on the right spiritual track. If the minister could not convince the dissenter of his error, the wayward person obviously was going against the light of his own conscience. There was no excuse for remaining in darkness after one's path had been illuminated by the Word, properly focused. This extreme biblicism permitted John Cotton to contend that while it was wrong to force a man to violate his own conscience, it was not wrong to force the truth upon him. Cotton extricated himself from that seeming contradiction by pointing out that "no man's con-science forced him to reject the truth and therefore to force the truth upon him was no violation of conscience."[14]

In a typical pithy description, Perry Miller refers to the Bay Company as an "organized task force of Christians, executing a flank attack on the corruptions of Christendom."[15] These Puritans did not flee to America; "they went in order to work out that complete reformation which was not yet accomplished in England and Europe, but which would be quickly accom-plished if only the saints back there had a working model to guide them."[16]

Miller contended that not only did the Puritans expect to succeed in their "errand into the wilderness," but they fully expected someday to return to England to govern that island of iniquity and restore it to its proper place in the Kingdom of God. The church-state in New England would serve as the prototype for all Europe to copy.

Miller argues with clarity and humor that Winthrop's revo-lutionaries intended to be only "temporary colonials." The prime purpose of the Puritans' errand was to set a city on a hill for all the world to see and imitate. But the actors on the New England stage lost their audience with the outbreak of the Civil Wars in England in the 1640s. The Puritans in America were further perplexed when the Puritan movement in England split between the Presbyterian and Independent factions. That meant no one model could serve a church divided into two equal parts. Then the Independents in England betrayed their brethren in America by "yielding to the heresy of toleration." They even embraced the religious rebel Roger Williams, who had been expelled from Massachusetts!

The tensions between the Independents on both sides of the Atlantic were further increased when, in Miller's humorous prose, "Oliver Cromwell was so far gone in his idiocy as to become a dictator, in order to impose toleration by force! Amid this shambles, the errand of New England collapsed. There was nobody left at headquarters to whom reports could be sent."[17]

At this point Americans had their first identity problem. If the Puritans in New England no longer had to work to maintain their "due form of government, civil and ecclesiastical, that they brought into being,"[18] then what were they about? Had God withdrawn His commission? Were they rebels without a cause?

The perplexed Puritans turned inward to search their hearts for the answer—and discovered a sinkhole of iniquity. Events had conspired to cast them upon "iron couches of introspection." The audience had filed out of the auditorium, the stage lights were turned off "and they were left alone with America."[19]

But the play was far from being over. Their purpose for building a city on a hill on which the world would rivet its attention may have changed, but build they would. God had promised never to leave them or forsake them if they had "the ordinances planted among them, and themselves planted into the ordinances."[20] If the New England model could not be transplanted to European soil, then at least those suffering persecution for their religious beliefs could come to America.

Religious liberty had fallen on hard times in Europe. Heretics were still being burned at the stake. America was a land of new beginnings. Here true religion could be practiced in its pristine beauty. The city set on the hill would be seen by all the world and serve as a beacon, rather than as a model. In decades to follow, thousands of immigrants would follow that beacon to a land big enough to accommodate all shades of religious beliefs. It wasn't what the original Puritan settlers had in mind, but then God has always moved in mysterious ways. And no one knew that better than the Puritans. "The God of the Covenant always remained an unpredictable Jehovah" whose ways are not to be questioned.[21] God doesn't make mistakes. He had not cancelled the divine drama still to be played on the American stage.

FIVE

The Holy Experiment

In the first century the Apostle Paul had written, "If any man be in Christ, he is a new creature" (2 Corinthians 5:17). By meditating on his own sinfulness and the unmerited grace of God displayed in the sacrificial death of Jesus Christ on the cross, the Puritan believed that the vilest sinner could experience the regenerating work of the Holy Spirit.

"The Puritan preachers sought nothing less than a new kind of Englishman," Sydney Ahlstrom asserts in his massive volume. "Their aims, to use a modern expression, were countercultural; their straightforward, earnest, plain-style sermons were meant to accomplish a 'revolution of the saints.' "[1]

More than a place of worship, the Puritan meetinghouse also served as a community center for social activity and political action. Town meetings could range from electing selectmen to settling the salary for the local minister.

A Dutch visitor to Plymouth, in 1627, describes how the Pilgrims' meetinghouse became the center of colonial life:

> Upon the hill they have a large square meeting-house, with
> a flat roof, made of thick, sawn planks, stayed with oak beams,

upon the top of which they have six cannons, which shoot iron balls of four and five pounds, and command the surrounding country. The lower part they use for their church, where they preach on Sundays and the usual holidays.

They assemble by beat of drums, each with his musket or firelock, in front of the captain's [Myles Standish's] door; they have their cloaks on, and place themselves in order, three abreast, and are led by a sergeant without beat of drum. Behind comes the Governor [William Bradford] in a long robe; beside him on the right hand, comes the preacher [Elder Brewster], with cloak on, and on the left hand the captain, with his side arms and cloak on, and with a small cane in his hand; and so they march in good order, and each sets his arms down near him.[2]

Who but proper Englishmen could pump so much pomp and pageantry into going to church?

An important part of the Dutch merchant's colorful account was the references to the Pilgrim Fathers taking their weapons to the worship service. One hundred and fifty years later, their descendants would use the pulpit as a platform from which to urge the men of their congregations to take up arms and march off to battle with the blessing of the church—and presumably God.

The fortress-church of Plymouth disappeared, of course, as the colonies became more thickly settled and the Indians were driven farther into the woods. Meetinghouses became small rectangular buildings—minus a steeple (which was regarded as a "popish" tower)—with the pulpit at one end. Puritan church services were segregated by social rank.

The Puritans would have shuddered at the comparison, but the New England church service developed into as much a ritual as the Catholic mass. As William Warren Sweet's description shows, a church bell or, in smaller towns, a drum

or conch shell summoned the entire community to worship.
The minister opened the service with a lengthy prayer, with
the people standing. Prayer was followed by Bible reading by
the minister, who commented on each passage. (To read the
Scripture without comment was looked upon as "dumb
reading," and only Anglican priests were guilty of that sin.)

The sermon, the centerpiece of the Puritan worship service,
generally lasted only an hour, except on special occasions,
when the minister would preach two or three hours.

Puritans were guilty of some of the most off-key singing
ever to mar a meeting of saints destined to spend eternity in
musical expression. The congregation sang Psalms, but they
only knew three or four different tunes. The ruling elder
"lined out" the Psalm in a seldom-successful attempt to keep
the congregation singing the same words at the same time. "I
myself have twice in one note paused to take breath," an
eighteenth-century New England minister confessed.

Sweet, in *The Story of Religion in America*, describes a
musical miscarriage when the members of a Puritan choir took
the deacon's instructions too literally:

> The story is told of a New England deacon who, because of
> failing eyesight, found difficulty in reading the first line of the
> Psalm and he apologized by observing: "My eyes, indeed, are
> very blind."
>
> The choir thinking this the first line of a common-meter
> hymn immediately sang it; whereupon the deacon exclaimed:
> "I cannot see at all."
>
> This the choir also sang. Astonished, the deacon cried out:
> "I really believe you are bewitched" and the choir responded,
> "I really believe you are bewitched," whereupon the deacon
> added, "The mischief's in you all," and after the choir had
> sung that, the deacon sat down in disgust.[3]

The church was the geographical center as well as the hub of social and political life. Radiating from the church was the common pasture, the village, the fields, and the farmlands.

A minister called to serve a congregation often held the post for his lifetime. He was ordained by the laying on of hands by the officers of the church representing the congregation. Some of the larger churches also hired a "teacher-elder"— associate pastor—to bring their spiritual organization up to full strength.

Separation of church and state never entered the minds of our Puritan forefathers. The general court (the legislative assembly) required that taxes be paid by the public to support the church. Political magistrates also were regarded as "nursing fathers" to defend the faith and protect the interest of the church. "The civil government also enforced the 'first table' of the Decalogue, punishing blasphemers, heresy and vain swearing, and requiring the Sabbath be kept."[4]

The Puritans obviously believed they had the best of both worlds with their "due forms" of ecclesiastical and civil governments. Urian Oakes, Cambridge minister and president of Harvard, believed it was clearly God's will for church and state to be one:

> According to the design of our founders and the frame of things laid by them, the interest of righteousness in the commonwealth and holiness in the Churches are inseparable . . . To divide what God hath conjoyned . . . is folly in its exaltation. I look upon this as a little model of the glorious kingdom of Christ on earth. Christ reigns among us in the commonwealth as well as in the church and hath his glorious interest involved and wrapt up in the good of both societies respectively."[5]

Puritans accepted the Calvinist doctrine that man was inherently sinful, impotent when it came to trying to work out his own salvation, and was saved by God's irresistible grace. The grace of God was extended to whom He elected. The Puritans continually worried whether they were recipients of God's grace, but worry was good for the soul, because it was a sign that one was on the road to being saved. The real danger signal was when one stopped worrying about his spiritual status.

Sweet, quoting Samuel Eliot Morison, contends the Puritans were not Predestinarian Calvinists. "The Puritan sermons assumed that salvation lay within the reach of all, by virtue of the Covenant of Grace and the efforts of the churches. The Puritan believed that each individual had his own place in a divinely ordered universe, and that God had a personal concern for him and his work, and it made no difference how humble he or it might be."[6] This theory contradicts the argument that fatalism dominated Puritan society.

In many ways, the Puritan was an optimist. He knew that God had created the earth and all that dwelled therein, and then had stepped back and called it good. True, sin had flawed God's good creation. But not to the point of ruin.

The Puritan was no ascetic. Many Puritans never drank water except as a last resort, preferring to quench their thirst with home brew. Spirits flowed freely on election day, a kind of holiday in New England. However, moderation was the theme, and pleasure was a by-product, never an end in itself.

The Puritan sanctified the secular. Indeed, he believed all "callings"—whether farmer, sea captain, merchant, or minister—were equally Christian. The Puritan temperament, disciplined life, and dedication to vocation, usually meant one achieved varying degrees of success in whatever endeavor was undertaken.

As Edmund Burke reminded his colleagues in the House of Commons on the outbreak of the American Revolution, religion was "always a principle of energy in this new people."

But the piety of this people eventually began to cool. In the last third of the seventeenth century, old-line Puritan leaders detected a diminishing of zeal and spiritual energy. Urian Oakes pinpointed the problem: The faithful had become "sermon proof." Inoculated with so many doses of orthodox sermons, they had become immune to catching the real thing—orthodox Christianity. A "cooling of former life and heate in spiritual communion" occurred. Religious formality, high morals, and intellectual assent to orthodox beliefs replaced experiential piety. The beat was missing in religion of the heart. Souls were not being stirred. "There is risen up a generation," lamented Increase Mather, in 1674, "who give out, as if saving grace and Morality were the same."[7] The regenerative power of the Holy Spirit experienced by the fathers was not being visited on the second generation—and who would dare predict what would happen in the third and fourth generations!

The indifference of the second generation of Puritans toward "matters of the heart" called for adjustments in church membership. Charter members of the New England Congregational churches had been adults who testified to a transforming, personal Christian experience. The promises of the covenant, however, also took in the children of the redeemed. Many of these baptized children grew up in the church, lived lives above reproach, and attended all the required services, but never had the same kind of personal experience that had made "visible saints" of their parents. The second generation of Puritans, however, wanted their children to be admitted to church membership—there were obvious temporal advantages as well as spiritual benefits. The strict constructionists of the covenant contended that only the immediate offspring of saved saints could receive the sacrament of baptism. The more liberal element wanted to compromise: Permit the children of unregenerate but baptized members who owned the covenant to be baptized but ban them from voting in church affairs and taking Holy Communion.

The issue divided New England churches for more than a decade. The Massachusetts general court called for all the churches to meet in Boston in March of 1662 and settle the matter once for all. The "grandfather clause"—as Marion L. Starkey so aptly described the compromise which permitted grandchildren of the elect to be baptized but not partake of communion[8]—carried the day. The liberals may have won the battle, but the war was far from being over.

The Brattle Street Church accepted the principle of the Half-Way Covenant on the basis that "we dare not refuse it [baptism] to any child offered to us by a professed Christian [whether or not in full communion with the church] upon his engagement to see it educated, if God give life and ability, in the Christian Religion."[9]

President Increase Mather of Harvard (that bastion of orthodoxy) exploded in holy fury. "To admit persons 'orthodox in judgment' as to matter of faith and 'not scandalous in life' to partake of the Lord's Supper 'without an examination concerning the work of grace in their hearts' would be a real apostasy from former principles, and a degeneracy from the Reformation."[10]

Mather was fighting a rearguard action. In 1700, the Reverend Solomon Stoddard, pastor of the frontier community in Northampton, Massachusetts, and a spiritual dictator of the first water, engaged President Mather in a protracted controversy. Stoddard added a new twist to the Half-Way Covenant. Stoddard held that children of nonsaints should not only be permitted to be baptized but also accepted at the

Lord's Table. Stoddard argued that Holy Communion could lead one into a conversion experience.

According to one story, which surfaced after the grand old man's death, Stoddard himself came to Northampton, correct in doctrine and adequately prepared to preach, but still unconverted. His wife decided to remedy that defect by calling the ladies of the community to pray for her husband's salvation. Stoddard learned about the intercession going on in his behalf and was plunged into deep thought.

"Not long after, in the act of serving communion to his congregation, his soul was suddenly flooded with a sense of divine well being that he had not known before. For the first time he entered the emotional reality of conversion, and since it happened at the Lord's Table, he came to the belief that others should share this opportunity."[11]

It may have worked that way for Stoddard, but it didn't for others. The relaxation of church-admission standards opened the floodgate to the unconverted and unfit. The church became spiritually flabby.

The perceptive Increase Mather could read the handwriting on the wall. The saints of New England were not holding up their end of the holy covenant. God's displeasure was manifest in such sure signs as a smallpox scourge, King Phillip's War, and two fires, which ravaged Boston in 1676 and 1679.

These "acts of God" called for a time of soul-searching and self-examination by the Puritan leaders to try to find out what they had been doing wrong. They knew God chastises His Chosen People only to correct them because He loves them.

The General Court of Massachusetts, under Mather's prodding, called a reforming synod of 1679. Mather was elected president, and under his leadership the synod called on the local churches to be more strict in church discipline and more careful in executing the laws of the colony. A confession of faith also was adopted. The delegates to the synod must have left rejoicing that they had remedied the conditions that had triggered God's wrath.

The worst was yet to come. In October, 1684, five years after the synod, the British Court of Chancery revoked Massachusetts' original charter. In 1685 the newly crowned James II wanted to tighten his control over the American colonies and did so by placing them under the jurisdiction of a royal governor. Sir Edmund Andros was sent to Boston in 1686 to carry out the king's plan. He initially was appointed governor of Massachusetts, Maine, New Hampshire, and Plymouth. His authority later extended to Connecticut, Rhode Island, New Jersey, and New York. Popular rights were abolished. The colonies even lost their power of taxation and freedom of the press.[12]

Governor Andros further infuriated the colonists when he inserted the Established Church into the inner sanctum of the Holy Commonwealth. The governor did ask for permission to hold Anglican services in one of the meetinghouses when it was not in use for services by the owners. The Congregationalists of course would not permit such an abomination. Andros then appropriated the Old South Meeting House and held Anglican services there on Good Friday and Easter, 1687. The following year work began on the first Anglican church in Massachusetts—King's Chapel.[13] Americans were to hear more from the Anglicans in years to come.

Andros had a short reign. When the Catholic King James II was forced from the throne by the Protestants in England, Americans rejoiced. Governor Andros was clapped in prison, and the home-rule impulse of the Americans expressed itself in a provisional government set up until they could obtain a new charter.[14]

President Increase Mather, one of the first of a long line of

Harvard men to answer the call to civil service, was chosen, with three others, to go to England to negotiate for a new charter. They secured a charter in 1691, and Mather's powers of persuasion are reflected in the fact that he was given the right to nominate those who should first take office under it.

However, the new charter was not a copy of the original. The most fundamental change was the elimination of religious qualifications required to vote. The franchise now would be based on property rights rather than religious experience. The crown would continue to appoint the governor. Only the lower house of the legislature would be elected by the popular vote.

The new charter broke the Puritan hammerlock on the administration of political affairs in New England. With the jealously guarded privileges of the saints swept away, a new order had begun.

Liberalizing trends took place across the Puritan landscape. Even Harvard College showed signs of erosion around her orthodox foundations. Connecticut churches tried to cut their spiritual losses by founding a new college named after Elihu Yale, who gave the largest gift.

Power shifts also took place in the local congregations. Authority seemed to flow toward the pulpit, and the preachers gratefully accepted all the power they could get. Ministerial associations were formed to expand and preserve the power shift. Under the guise of advocating administrative reform, the associations arrogated to themselves the right to examine and license candidates for the ministry. The associations also developed into a kind of union hiring hall for clergy.

Connecticut churches gradually drifted more toward the Presbyterian form of church government than did the churches in Massachusetts, which continued to honor the independence of the local congregation.

The attention given to church polity reflected the spiritual anemia that had subtly invaded the churches. Religion had become more and more a matter of the head rather than of the heart. William Warren Sweet's summary is especially apt:

> The Puritan fathers had held that conversion was solely the work of God, but with the second and third generations, as the number of conversions decreased, gradually the idea began to emerge that there were certain "means" which might be used in putting the soul in a position to receive the regenerating influence of the Spirit of God. Such "means" were owning the covenant, attending divine worship, leading a moral life, reading the Scriptures and prayer. Thus there came to be more and more reliance upon the use of "means" and less and less upon the miraculous power of God, which led to a cold and unemotional religion."[15]

Twenty-five years before the first shots heard around the world were fired, one of these champions of a religion based on reason would preach a fiery sermon that would become "the morning gun of the revolution." One hears more about Patrick Henry than the Reverend Jonathan Mayhew. But that intellectual preacher with Puritan roots set forth principles that would later be used to justify the break with England.

Mayhew represents a rational religious stream that flowed into the more emotional waters roiled by the Great Awakening. The two surged together into an irresistible rolling river that would overflow and sweep away the political ties that bound the United States to England.

The lights in the city set on a hill began to dim. But a closer look revealed it was merely the footlights that had been turned down. An original drama, called *The Birth of a Nation*, was about to unfold.

SIX

"The Morning Gun of the Revolution"

The name *Reverend Jonathan Mayhew* is hardly a household word, even among history students. Yet this man, regarded by many of his contemporaries as the "master spirit" of the Revolution,[1] powerfully influenced the tiny band of radicals whom King George unsuccessfully tried to ban from Boston and helped arouse, educate, and mold the minds of the masses.

John Adams listed Mayhew as one of the five "first and foremost" patriots who produced the great political awakening that made the Revolution possible. Adams's first two choices were James Otis and Oxenbridge Thacher, the two lawyers who pleaded the case of the merchants in the Superior Court of Massachusetts. Then came Sam Adams and John Hancock. Jonathan Mayhew was the fifth "foremost" patriot in Adams's quintet.

Adams overflowingly praised Mayhew, calling the Congregationalist clergyman a "Whig of the first magnitude—a clergyman equalled by very few of any denomination in piety, virtue, genius of learning; whose works will maintain his character as long as New England shall be free, integrity esteemed, or wit, spirit, humor, reason and knowledge admired."[2]

Jonathan Mayhew came from a long line of preacher-farmers who lived on Martha's Vineyard, where he was born on October 8, 1720. He graduated, in 1744, from Harvard College, where he distinguished himself with the ease with which he wrote Latin and the eloquence with which he spoke the King's English.

He was awarded the prominent pulpit in Boston's West Church three years after he graduated and held that prestigious post until his death in 1766.

Mayhew was a controversialist even during his student days at Harvard, and his radical religious beliefs caused him to be suspect in the eyes of the orthodox clergy of Boston. Mayhew had the theological audacity to spurn the basic tenets of Calvinist theology. Even more offensive to his colleagues was the fact he reveled in his "incipient heresy." He openly denied the deity of Jesus Christ and rejected the doctrine of the Trinity.

Mayhew has been called the first Unitarian. If he did not deserve the title in life, he earned it posthumously. His legacy of religious liberalism caused West Church to be the first congregation in that region to declare itself as Unitarian.

Mayhew's sermons, "frequently flung into print and scattered hither and yon in this country and England,"[3] read as if they were etched in acid. Satire was his forte. As a liberal, he had a closed mind when it came to evangelical Christianity. After condescending to listen to the eloquent evangelist George Whitefield, Mayhew wrote his father: "It was as low, confused, puerile, conceited, ill-natured, enthusiastic a performance as I ever heard."[4]

The description of Mayhew by the author of *The Literary History of the Revolution* may have been overblown, but it obviously has more than a touch of truth in it:

> A robust and fiery antagonist of almost every form of arbitrary authority in church or state; a man of such boldness of character, splendor of diction, wit, sarcasm, invective, of such enthusiasm for all spacious and breezy views of freedom and duty, that he had become sort of a tribune of the people— particularly, the companion and inspirer of many of those young radicals in politics who, long before the final onset of the American Revolution, were unconsciously beating out a path for it.[5]

Mayhew never bothered developing the Christian virtues of charity and humility "which he had to content himself with eloquently commending to the practice of others." Others less kind, perceived him as a preacher of "haughty spirits and vanity."[6]

Mayhew was a true son of the Enlightenment. "Our anointed Lord," he asserted, "the author and finisher of our faith, constantly appealed to the senses and the reason of mankind. . . ."[7] He even drained the love of God of all emotion and distilled it into a "steady, solemn, calm and rational thing, the result of thought and consideration. It is, indeed, a passion, but a passion excited by reason presenting the proper object of it to the mind."[8]

The arid, rational brain of Jonathan Mayhew refused to register any emotions even when jolted by an earthquake. Once, after Boston had been shaken by two quakes in three days, most ministers exhorted the wicked to repent and the righteous to awake from their spiritual slumbers. But Mayhew assured his congregation that he was not going to exploit the situation "when the minds of so many people may be ruffled and discomposed, to promote the cause of superstition. . . . I shall therefore address myself to you as men and *reasonable* creatures."[9] So he did.

The radical Puritan preacher also cloaked his sermons in the "very garb of rebellion," and his congregation never slept. The manner in which Mayhew communicated ideas often made a greater impact than the contents of his message. Alice Baldwin wrote that by the time the Declaration of Independence was signed, in 1776, Puritan preachers had taught "the right to life, liberty, and property" for more than one hundred years.[1] But none preached resistance more boldly or more passionately than the firebrand Jonathan Mayhew.

A born rebel, Mayhew made his colleagues of the cloth feel uneasy because of his unorthodox views. He was arrogant, aggressive, and attractive. His flamboyant style and radical ideas appealed to the avant-garde Boston liberals. His sermons were studies in eloquence. In them Mayhew quickly sounded the alarm over what he perceived as the erosion of American rights by British officialdom—ecclesiastical or civil. "People are not usually deprived of their liberties all at once," he warned in one sermon, "but gradually, by one encroachment after another."[11]

Attired in a black, ankle-length robe, the Reverend Jonathan Mayhew must have found it difficult to suppress a sneer as he solemnly mounted his pulpit at the West Church, in Boston, on January 30, 1750—the one hundred and first anniversary of the beheading of King Charles I by Cromwell and his zealous Puritan Parliament. High-church Royalists had canonized the dead king as an Anglican martyr, and the anniversary of King Charles's execution had been declared a day of fasting and repentance, to give English subjects the opportunity to atone for their collective guilt in killing a king. Every Church of England priest was compelled to read the Oxford homily against "disobedience and willful rebellion, or to preach a sermon against that sin."[12]

As a dissenting clergyman in rebellious Boston, Mayhew could not be expected to extoll the virtues of the dead monarch. In fact, Mayhew admitted that in part "the senseless clamor of some Tory-spirited churchmen"[13] had provoked his sermon.

Mayhew did not aim his sermon so much at tyrants as at Anglican priests who preached nonresistance and unlimited submission to tyrants. The colonist had no quarrel with the then-reigning King George II, and Mayhew would go to an early grave before the colonists ever seriously considered resisting King George III. But dealing a death blow to the Anglican canard of nonresistance on a fast day commemorating the death of a tyrant king was just the type of twist at which Mayhew excelled. The thirty-year-old radical preacher-patriot would gladly go the second mile in order to heap fiery coals on the crowned and mitered heads of English kings and Anglican bishops.

The sermon itself went by the laborious title, "Discourse Concerning Unlimited Submission and Non-Resistance to the Higher Powers," with the subtitle, "With Some Reflections on the Resistance Made to King Charles I and on the Anniversary of His Death, in which the Mysterious Doctrine of that Prince's Saintship and Martyrdom is Unriddled."

The sermon was so politically potent that admiring historian John Wingate Thornton called it "the morning gun of the revolution."[14] Thus fifteen years before Patrick Henry was warned to bite his tongue in the House of Burgesses, because he was talking treason, a Boston preacher served notice that America would never accept "lords spiritual" (bishops) or "tyrants temporal" (kings) who attempted to deprive colonists of their divine rights of civil and religious freedom. The widely acclaimed champion of civil and religious freedom warned his countrymen of "an impious bargain struck up betwixt the sceptre and the surplice for enslaving both the bodies and souls of men."[15] Whether this charge had any substance didn't really matter to most colonists; the possibility alone caused them to shudder.

Mayhew vehemently opposed any suggestion of settling Anglican bishops in America. In the eighteenth century Dissenters saw Anglican bishops as religious "secret agents" for the English monarchy. "Crown and scepter" formed an unholy alliance in the minds of Independents, whose ancestors had fled England because their religious freedom was being stifled.

Mayhew viewed the establishment of an episcopacy in the colonies as the first step by the Church of England to gain political control of the American political assemblies. Once in the political saddle, the Royalists could impose religious tests, as they had in England, for political appointments and civil offices. That would leave the Nonconformists with only the crumbs from the bishops' tables. "Anglican bishops became the principal symbol in the American mind of the threatened ecclesiastical tyranny."[16]

So a desire to war with Anglicanism spurred the pugnacious Mayhew to preach his classical political sermon on unlimited submission. The ideas expressed in the sermon were ten years ahead of their time, a kind of storm signal pointing to the intense debate over religious and civil liberty that would sweep the Atlantic seaboard in the 1760s.

The Episcopal clergy in America treated the beheading of King Charles as a form of deicide. "The most excreable murder ever committed since that of our blessed Saviour!"

one high-church Anglican exclaimed.[17] Episcopal clergymen used the fast day to exalt the superiority of episcopacy and the divine right of kings while downgrading republican principles and the Congregational church system. Servile sermons preached in Episcopal pulpits called for absolute submission and nonresistance to the king.

The Puritan clergy responded by proving from Scripture that Christ had called men to be free of the yoke of civil and religious tyranny; they used the gospel as a prop to buttress partisan political positions. Scripturally spiced sermons often degenerated into bitter polemics. Among a population steadily being propelled into a war proclaimed by Puritan preachers to be a holy crusade, charity became the first victim.

Mayhew's sermon is not easy reading, with its long and at times convoluted sentences. In the reasoned, logical argument and the formal style of the eighteenth-century preacher, he lacerated his enemies, with carefully chosen words, wit, satire, and irony. He obviously enjoyed the sound of his own rhetoric.

As his text Mayhew took the passage most often cited by those who preached unlimited submission and nonresistance to the monarch—Romans 13:1–8, a passage used by those favoring the status quo for countless centuries. The opening verses state: "Let every soul be subject unto the higher powers. For there is no power but of God: the powers that be are ordained of God. Whosoever therefore resisteth the power, resisteth the ordinance of God: and they that resist shall receive to themselves damnation."

Mayhew would stand the passage on its head to make it come out the way he wanted. A brilliant preacher, he could exegete with the best of theologians. He had a political point to make, and Scripture would serve as a stepping-stone for advancing his argument.

"I beg it may be remembered," Mayhew began, "that 'all Scripture is profitable for doctrine, for reproof, for correction, for instruction in righteousness.' " Having laid down a principle that no one in Puritan Boston could challenge, Mayhew then plunged ahead to hoist his critics on their own petard. "Why, then," he asked, "should not those parts of Scripture which relate to civil government be examined and explained from the desk [pulpit], as well as others?"[18] Thus the rationalist Mayhew, who believed God could be better known through His works than through His Word, had taken the "high ground" of proof texting, silencing his opponents with Scripture.

Mayhew placed the passage in its proper historical context by explaining that the letter to the Roman Christians was written by Paul because some first-century believers held the mistaken notion that as citizens of heaven they were not subject to earthly rulers. They argued that because of their "subjection to Christ, they were wholly freed from subjection to any other prince."

Mayhew, no anarchist, believed that government was ordained of God. But as did all Puritan divines, versed in the political philosophy of John Locke, he believed that rulers ruled at the will of the people. The question then was not whether a Christian should submit to authority, but to what *extent* does one submit?

Mayhew cited the Old Testament to prove that the prevailing European belief in the divine right of kings not only contradicted God's law but stemmed from sin in the first place. "God does not interpose in a miraculous way to point out the persons who shall bear rule, and to whom submission is due," he commented sarcastically. "And as to the unalienable, indefeasible right of primogeniture, the Scriptures are entirely silent or, rather, plainly contradict it, Saul being the

first King among the Israelites, and appointed to the royal
dignity during his father's lifetime; and he was succeeded, or
rather superceded by 'David, the last born among many
brethren.' "

Keep in mind that Mayhew's sermon preceded King George
III's accession to the throne by ten years. In 1750, the
American colonies could protest the policies of Great Britain,
but *independence* was a word still to be applied by Sam Adams.
Mayhew was attempting to justify a revolution that took place
one hundred years before, in England, which resulted in the
beheading of the king. But in his zeal, he also laid a biblical
basis for a war that would take place twenty-five years later, in
America. Historian Perry Miller correctly calls Mayhew the
"most obvious link between Puritan and revolutionary
ideas."[19]

Having made the argument that God instituted government
among men to promote their general welfare but did not
specify the form, Mayhew argued that men must adopt a form
of government of their own choosing. To Mayhew, that
meant a government by social compact, a political principle
calling for the right of men to choose their own rulers. The
ruler was limited, because the people had the right to give
authority and to take it away—and by violence if necessary.

In effect, this compact merely transferred Congregational
polity into the political realm. In theory, the Puritan preacher
served at the pleasure of the congregation and could be
dismissed by them. But it didn't always work that way in
practice. Many preachers developed into spiritual dictators
through the sheer force of their personalities and the respect
accorded them as God's spokesmen on earth.

Mayhew believed that God Himself is limited by the terms
of the covenant, or contract, that He entered into with His
people. As Perry Miller points out, "To this enlightened

Puritan [Mayhew]. . . . The advantage to be derived from corporate existence is no longer the salvation but the well-being of the citizen. The power even of the Puritan God—and therefore, naturally that of an English King—is bound by the terms of the compact. New England's errand into the wilderness—having set out from the federal [or covenant] theology—has now developed into an assurance that God Himself would respect the laws we have agreed upon."[20]

If God cannot go beyond certain boundaries He has agreed upon in His compact with His Chosen People, then rest assured that no earthly king dare meddle with the rights of free men.

Mayhew contended there are conditions possible in which resistance would be justified: "Some have thought it warrantable and glorious to disobey the civil powers in certain circumstances, and in cases of very great and general oppression, when humble remonstrances fail of having any effect, and when the public welfare can not be otherwise provided for and secured, to rise unanimously even against the sovereign himself in order to redress their grievances, to vindicate their natural and legal rights, to break the yoke of tyranny, and free themselves and posterity from inglorious servitude and ruin.

"It is upon this principle that Tarquin was expelled from Rome, and Julius Caesar, the conqueror of the world and the tyrant of his country, cut off in the Senate house. It was upon this principle that King Charles I was beheaded before his own banqueting house. It was upon this principle that King James II was made to fly that country which he aimed at enslaving; and upon this principle was that revolution brought about which has been so fruitful of happy consequences to Great Britain."

One can almost see the young radical minister's lips curl in derision as he lashed out at the Anglican policy of unlimited submission: "But in opposition to this principle [unlimited submission], it has often been asserted that the Scriptures in general, and the passage under consideration in particular, make all resistance to princes a crime, in any cases whatever. If they turn tyrants and become the common oppressors of those whose welfare they ought to regard with a paternal affection, we must not pretend to right ourselves, unless it be by prayers, and tears and humble entreaties. And if these methods fail of procuring redress, we must not have recourse to any other, but all suffer ourselves to be robbed and butchered at the pleasure of the 'Lord's anointed' lest we should incur the sin of rebellion and the punishment of damnation!—for he has God's authority and commission to bear him out in the worst of crimes so far that he may not be withstood or controlled."

Mayhew conceded that one passage in the New Testament "at first view" seems to enjoin unlimited submission to civil rulers. He quoted the verse "Submit yourselves to every ordinance of man for the Lord's sake. . ." (1 Peter 2:13). The minister went on to emphasize that the key phrase of the verse is "every ordinance of man." That means Christians are to submit themselves to "every order of magistrates appointed by man, whether superior or inferior . . . to such ordinances and commands as are not *inconsistent* with the ordinances and commands of God, the Supreme Lawgiver, or with any higher and antecedent obligations. . . ."

Having disposed of Peter, he turned back to Paul and his text in Romans 13 for what the Puritan divines called the "hinge" of his argument: What Paul called for, Mayhew contended, was not submission "to *all*" rulers "but *only*" to those rulers who exercise "a reasonable and just authority for the good of human society. . . ." Does not the passage itself state that "rulers are not a terror to good works, but to the evil. . . . For He is the minister of God to thee for good. . ."? (Romans 13:3, 4.)

"It is obvious, then," Mayhew continued, "in general, that the civil rulers whom the apostle here speaks of, and obedience to whom he presses upon Christians as a duty, are good rulers, such as are, in the exercise of their office and power, benefactors to society." From the Anglican point of view Mayhew had turned the passage upside down.

"It is manifest," he thundered, "that this character and description of rulers agrees only to such as are rulers in fact as well as in name, to such as govern well, and act agreeably to their office. And the Apostle's argument for submission is wholly built and grounded upon a presumption that they do in fact answer this character.

"If rulers are a terror to good works and not to the evil; if they are not ministers for good to society but for evil and distress by violence and oppression; if they execute wrath upon sober, peaceable persons who do their duty as members of society, and suffer rich and honorable knaves to escape with impunity; if instead of attending continually upon the good work of advancing the public welfare—if this be the case, it is plain that the Apostle's argument for submission does not reach them."

Mayhew moved from proving that Scripture did not require unlimited submission to the logical next step—rulers turned tyrants were to be resisted. It was in fact unchristian not to resist.

"Rulers have no authority from God to do mischief. . . . It is blasphemy to call tyrants and oppressors God's ministers. They are more properly 'the messengers of Satan to buffet us.' No rulers are properly God's ministers but such as are 'just, ruling in the fear of God.' When once magistrates act contrary to their office and to the end of their institutions—when they rob and ruin the public instead of being guardians of its peace and welfare—they immediately cease to be ordinance and ministers of God, and no more deserve that glorious character than common pirates and highwaymen.

"If it be our duty, for example, to obey our king merely for this reason, that he rules for the public welfare (which is the only argument the apostle makes use of), it follows, by a parity of reason, that when he turns tyrant and makes his subjects his prey to devour and destroy, instead of his charge to defend and cherish, *we are bound to throw off our allegiance to him and to resist;* And that according to the tenor of the apostle's argument in this passage. . . .

"It is true," Mayhew concluded, "the apostle puts no case of such a tyrannical prince, but, by his grounding this argument for submission wholly upon the good of civil society, it is plain he implicitly authorizes, and even *requires* us to make resistance, whenever, this shall be necessary to the public safety and happiness."

Mayhew summarized his arguments, "We may safely assert these two things in general, without undermining government: One is, that no civil rulers are to be obeyed when they enjoin things that are inconsistent with the commands of God. All such disobedience is lawful and glorious; particularly if persons refuse to comply with any legal *establishment* of religion, because it is a gross perversion and corruption—as to doctrine, worship and discipline—of a pure and divine religion, brought from heaven to earth by the Son of God—the only King and Head of the Christian church—and propagated through the world by his inspired apostles."

It seems rather ironic that Mayhew would attack the legal establishment of religion—obviously with the Church of England in mind—when his own Congregational denomination was established in Massachusetts, Connecticut, and New Hampshire, and he was thus speaking from an establishment pulpit.

Mayhew warned in his sermon, however, that men should not rush into revolution every time a ruler makes a mistake. "Now as all men are fallible," he said, "it cannot be supposed that the public affairs of any state should always be administered in the best manner possible, even by persons of the greatest wisdom and integrity.

"Nor is it sufficient to legitimate disobedience to the higher powers that they are not so administered, or that they are in some instances very ill-managed; for upon this principle, it is scarcely supposable that any government at all could be supported, or subsist.

"Such a principle manifestly tends to the dissolution of government, and to throw all things into confusion and anarchy. But it is equally evident, upon the other hand, that those in authority may abuse their trust and power to such a degree, that neither the law of reason nor of religion requires that any obedience or submission should be paid to them; but, on the contrary, that they should be totally discarded, and the authority which they were before vested with transferred to others, who may exercise it more to those good purposes for which it is given."

After devastating the Anglican argument of unlimited submission and absolute nonresistance and after carefully building a case justifying the execution of the "wicked" King Charles, Mayhew ended his sermon on a strangely subdued note.

In 1750, the colonists reveled in the fact that the Hanoverians were on the throne in London. The Georges were good Protestant kings, in contrast to the unhappy reign of the Stuarts. Mayhew ended his sermon with an appeal to all men to respect rulers and to remember that "government is sacred and not to be trifled with."

As if to prove that a dissenting clergyman could be a loyal subject, he affirmed: "It is our happiness to live under a prince [King George II] who is satisfied with ruling according to law, as every other good prince will. We enjoy under his administration all the liberty that is proper and expedient for us. It becomes us, therefore, to be contented and dutiful subjects."

But Mayhew's verbal genuflection toward the throne failed to defuse the political dynamite burning in his sermon. The sermon sent shock waves rolling across Tory-minded churchmen in New England, who flooded Boston newspapers with abusive articles and caustic comments. The day after the sermon was given, one Anglican priest, reading the signs of the time, wrote to his bishop in England that the need for an American-based bishop was now greater than ever before. Boston's four newspapers gave the sermon and reaction to it page-one play.

Mayhew walked from the pulpit on that Sunday in January of 1750 as the newly crowned champion of freedom. The eyes of Boston—and those in the hinterland—were upon the young, flaming radical. Even his fellow ministers had to admit a new leader had arisen in the land. But they still would not accept him as a member in the Boston Association of Ministers.

For six months, the *Boston Evening Post* filled its columns with attacks on and answers to Mayhew's sermon. One contributor said his article was in response to "a certain wrangling Preacher in this Town" for "having belched out a Flood of Obloquy" upon King Charles. "One article warned the public in a comparison of the tenth of January (Charles' birthday) with the thirtieth of the same month (his execution)

immediately suggested 'the great danger of the State, whenever the Ecclesiastical Government is struck at: or in other
words it naturally leads us to believe, that *the fall of the crown
is never any farther distant from that of the mitre*, than the
thirtieth of January is from the tenth, and therefore the Good
Old Saying, *no bishop, no king*, however grating it may be to
some people, ought to be the standing maxim of the English
Government.' "[21]

Mayhew had touched a politically sensitive nerve. Both
Dissenters and Anglicans were aware that the Church of
England sat at the right hand of the throne—a strategic
position in which to gain the ear of the king. The Dissenters
would not let that arrangement be transplanted to American
soil.

Mayhew believed, as did all Puritan preachers, that civil as
well as religious rights came from God, the Giver of all good
gifts. Englishmen, for so the colonists called themselves,
lived under a constitution, and every act of government had to
conform to that constitution, which was, in effect, the political
covenant. Their Bibles assured them they had the legal and
divine right to resist. It was a belief Mayhew would put into
action in his own life and one that would influence others long
after his death.

SEVEN

"A Communion of Colonies"

Not only did the words of Jonathan Mayhew's sermon set off wildfire among Dissenters and Anglicans in his own day, but they also fired the tongues and pens of the men who, years later, would form the spearhead of independence.

Mayhew was a close friend of one of Boston's most fiery revolutionaries, James Otis, Jr. Both Mayhew and Otis were passionate political orators, often indiscreet, combative, and long-winded.

Otis won the hearts of Bostonians—and a place in the history books—with his courtroom attack on the British writs of assistance. The writs permitted British customs officials to search ships and invade private homes or any other premises for smuggled goods. These writs posed a definite threat to Boston merchants who believed smuggling to be an essential part of the American free-enterprise system. John Hancock's ships sailed the Atlantic boldly and brazenly loaded with foreign goods on which no legal duty would ever be paid. Bribery was the acceptable way of getting customs officials to turn their heads. When these officials were finally forced to crack down on the smugglers, Boston merchants became outraged. Otis and his colleague, Oxenbridge Thacher, were retained to get the writs revoked by the Superior Court in Massachusetts, in 1761.

The two attorneys were opposites in style. Thacher quietly argued points of law, while the flamboyant Otis, in a tidal wave of rhetoric, denounced the writs as being unconstitutional. Otis, described by the *Boston Evening Post* as a "plump, round-faced, smooth-skinned, short necked, eagle-eyed politician," obviously was aware of the standing-room-only crowd jammed into the Council Room of the Boston Town House.

Otis lost his case. The defeat must have been doubly bitter, because an old political enemy of Otis's—Chief Justice Thomas Hutchinson—handed down the decision. But Otis's oratory so aroused the ire of the increasingly rebellious Boston patriots that it became impossible for customs officials to carry out their duties. The roar of the mob had gradually replaced the calm voice of constitutional authority.

John Adams, reminiscing about the origins of the Revolution, credited Otis with being the midwife to the child Independence. "Then and there," Adams wrote of Otis's courtroom delivery, "the child Independence was born. Then and there was the first scene of the first act of opposition to the arbitrary claims of Great Britain."[1]

Mayhew's close association with Otis demonstrates how clergymen influenced those political leaders who were pushing the colonies toward a rupture with the crown. In fact, ministers gave powerful shoves themselves.

Sam Adams took credit for first proposing the idea of joining all seacoast colonies into a union by setting up committees of correspondence. "This is a sudden thought and drops undigested from my pen," he wrote Arthur Lee in the fall of 1771.[2]

Actually, Jonathan Mayhew beat Adams to the punch by five years. The idea came to Mayhew more in the form of an intuitive flash rather than as a rational plan percolated through his lively intellectual processes. Mayhew said in his letter to Otis that the concept came to him while he was in bed on the "Lord's Day Morning [Sunday], June 8th, 1766.

"To a good man all time is holy enough," Mayhew wrote, "and none is too holy to do good, or to think upon it." In other words, thinking political thoughts on a Sunday morning was a legitimate spiritual exercise.

"Would it not be proper and decorous for our assembly to send circulars to all the rest, on the late repeal of the Stamp Act and the present favorable aspects of affairs?" Mayhew asked. He explained that because of the goodwill now flowing both ways across the Atlantic, the circular letters "should [be] conceived at once in terms of friendship and regard of loyalty to the king [whose popularity was at an all-time high then in the colonies] and filial affection towards the parent country, and expressing a desire to cement and perpetuate *union* among ourselves, by all laudable methods. . . ."

The colonies would do well to copy the pattern already being followed by the churches, Mayhew believed. "You have heard of the communion of churches," he reminded Otis. "While I was thinking of this in my bed, the great use and importance of a communion of colonies appeared to me in a strong light; which led me immediately to set down these hints to transmit to you."[3]

It was not the first time a preacher had been quicker than a politician in pointing out practical ways to further the common cause of the colonies. Ministers continually discussed the purpose and origins of government in sermons and gained practical political experience working within the framework of church government. It was a logical step from the concept of "communion of churches" to "communion of colonies."

But Sam Adams had other uses for the committees of correspondence than promoting loyalty to the king and "filial affection" toward the mother country. In 1771 and 1772, it looked as if the hotheads of Boston were going to be rebels without a cause. The British troops were gone. Parliament had repealed the Townshend Revenue Act, which had proved unworkable. True, the duty had been retained on tea, but that seemed insignificant at the time—although later it would become a central issue. It looked as if relations between England and her American colonies were drifting back toward a period of normalcy. The controversy over how to govern the colonies was not even an issue in the House of Commons for nearly eighteen months. Agitators in Boston found themselves more and more rehashing stale arguments—and then nobody seemed to be listening.

Obviously Sam Adams was losing his political clout. Even John Hancock became increasingly cool toward his old political mentor. Hancock's frustrated military ambition had been partly realized with his appointment as colonel of the Boston Cadets. His ego kept him from recognizing that the honor had been bestowed on him by the Tory Governor Thomas Hutchinson to wean the merchant-smuggler away from the Sons of Liberty. However, Sam Adams was made of sterner stuff. Worldly honors would not turn his head. He was not about to let the flame of resistance flicker out.

So Adams and his friends began making plans for colony-wide committees of correspondence. In November of 1772, the Boston town meeting created a standing committee of correspondence. James Otis was named chairman, although he did not have much faith in the efficacy of the committees.

Besides, Sam Adams was named secretary and used that post to determine the committee's agenda.

The idea caught fire and quickly spread throughout the towns of Massachusetts. The committee in Boston was ordered to draft statements of colonial rights and grievances, which were sent to all the towns in the province.

In early 1773 Virginia patriots set up a Virginia committee of correspondence and, ironically, jumped ahead of Adams by suggesting that all the colonies follow suit. The ultimate effect was a national network over which the ideas and propaganda of the radicals could be broadcast. "This is the foulest, subtlest and most venomous serpent that ever issued from the egg of sedition," Daniel Leonard, a loyalist, warned in the *Massachusetts Gazette.*[4]

While the committees never were used to bring about reconciliation between England and her American colonies, they did help to "cement and perpetuate union among ourselves" as Mayhew had hoped they would. Colonies that had in the past feuded over boundaries and tariffs began cooperating.

Had Mayhew lived longer, most historians agree he would have been in the front ranks of the patriots. He surely would have given his blessing to using the committees as a national communication system through which news and Whig propaganda could be exchanged.

Historian Donald Barr Chidsey believes that had Mayhew lived a little longer—he died on July 9, 1766, at the peak of his powers, at the age of forty-six—he "might have thrust himself ahead of Samuel Adams as the political czar of Massachusetts, but in that case he would have found Adams working for him as diligently, as intelligently, as before. For the man was born to toil in the cause of Independence."[5]

There is no question that Mayhew's eloquence could move

men to action—and even destruction. A dramatic illustration of his way with words took place in 1765. On March 22, the hated Stamp Act, imposing duties on a wide range of legal and commercial documents, became law. Mobs took to the streets, strong-arming stamp agents and threatening to fit them with a new "liberty suit"—made of hot tar and prickly feathers.

On August 25, 1765, Mayhew preached a "fiery sermon on the text: I would they were cut off which trouble you."[6] The mob took him at his word and sacked the mansion of the then Lieutenant Governor Thomas Hutchinson. (Ironically, Hutchinson opposed the Stamp Act.) When arrested, one ringleader justified his actions on the grounds that he became so excited by Mayhew's sermon that he thought "he was doing God service."

In a letter dated September 3, 1765, Mayhew disavowed any responsibility for inciting a riot. "As to the sermon itself," he wrote, "I own it was composed in a high strain of liberty. . . . But certain I am, that no person could, without abusing & perverting it, take encouragement from it to go mobbing, or to commit such abominable outrages as were lately committed, in defiance of the laws of God and man. I did, in the most formal express manner, discountenance everything of that kind."[7]

It has been said that "more clearly than any other man in colonial New England, he [Mayhew] viewed the fight for 'private judgment' in religion and the fight for personal liberty in politics as one grand battle in which all patriots could join with a will."[8]

Years earlier Mayhew had given moral impetus to the "grand battle" with his political sermon on the anniversary of the beheading of Charles I. It was freighted with the kind of political dynamite that would go on exploding in the face of British officials and clergy until the actual shooting started in

1775. Perhaps its greatest impact, however, was felt in a document that would rock a colonial empire.

Many historians have pointed out that Mayhew's reasons for abolishing government, as defined in "Discourse, Concerning Unlimited Submission and Non-Resistance to the Higher Powers," were strikingly similar to the argument made by Thomas Jefferson when he penned the Declaration of Independence, twenty-six years later.

Jefferson followed the preacher's ideas when he wrote: "That to secure these Rights, Governments are instituted among Men, deriving their just powers from the consent of the governed. That whenever any Form of Government becomes destructive of these ends, it is the Right of the People to alter or abolish it, and to institute new Government, laying its foundation on such principles, and organizing its powers in such form, as to them shall seem most likely to effect their Safety and Happiness."

Mayhew also preceded Jefferson in pointing out that most men are willing to suffer injustices for long periods before taking up arms to rid themselves of tyrants. Mayhew had said in his sermon:

> Nor is this principle, that resistance to the higher powers is in some extraordinary cases justifiable, so liable to abuse as many persons seem to apprehend it. . . . While those who govern do it with any tolerable degree of moderation and justice, and in any good measure act up to their office and character by being public benefactors, the people will generally be easy and peaceable, and be rather inclined to flatter and adore than to insult and resist them. Till people find themselves greatly abused and oppressed by their governors, they are not apt to complain; and whenever they do, in fact, find themselves abused and oppressed they must be stupid *not* to complain.[9]

Jefferson sounded as if he were rewriting Mayhew's sermon when he stated in the Declaration of Independence:

> Prudence, indeed, will dictate that Government long established should not be changed for light and transient causes; and accordingly, all experience hath shewn, that mankind are more disposed to suffer, while evils are sufferable, than to right themselves by abolishing the forms to which they are accustomed. But when a long train of abuses and usurpations, pursuing invariable the same Object, evinces a design to reduce them under absolute Despotism, it is their right, it is their duty, to throw off such Government, and to provide new Guards for their future security.

Both Mayhew and Jefferson agreed that the people have the right to determine when oppression has reached the point that revolution is justifiable before a "candid world." But once again a preacher beat the politician into print. Mayhew's eloquence rose to new heights when he stormed the walls of tyranny:

> To say that subjects in general are not proper judges when their governors oppress them and play the tyrant, and when they defend their rights, administer justice impartially, and promote the public welfare, is as great treason as ever man uttered. 'T is treason, not against one single man, but the state—against the whole body politic; 't is treason against mankind, 't is treason against common sense, 't is treason against God. And this impious principle lays the foundation for justifying all the tyranny and oppression that ever any prince was guilty of. The people know for what end they set up and maintain their governors, and they are the proper judges when they execute their trust as they ought to do it.

Mayhew devoted a large section of his sermon to listing the crimes of Charles I, which led to the civil war of 1640 and to the king's eventual execution. Jefferson used the same technique in the Declaration of Independence, listing the complaints against King George III as the "causes" that led to the Revolution of 1776. The remarkable parallels one finds between Mayhew's sermons and Jefferson's masterpiece lend credence to the observation of Alice Baldwin that "there is not a right asserted in the Declaration of Independence which had not been discussed by the New England clergy before 1763."[10] None discussed those rights more eloquently or more fervently than Jonathan Mayhew.

EIGHT

"The Bishops Are Coming!"

If Paul Revere shouted as he rode across the Massachusetts countryside, he might better have cried "The bishops are coming! The bishops are coming!" Had leather-lunged Revere shouted *bishops*, he would have gotten the same reaction as he did to the word *British*.

The fiercely independent Congregationalist clergy and their New England hierarchy-hating flocks saw bishops of the Church of England as thorns in the flesh of the body politic and the Body of Christ. The Dissenters who populated the eastern seaboard were radical religionists and political nonconformists of long standing, and Americans had become suspicious—to the point of being paranoid—of British motives and policies. Resistance to royalty had developed into an American trait—a colonial characteristic that the British, 3,000 miles away, either failed to discern or stubbornly ignored. But those with clear vision, such as far-sighted Member of Parliament Edmund Burke could see and understand what was happening and urged England to come to terms with their stiff-necked offspring. Burke's "Speech for Conciliation With the Colonies," delivered March 22, 1775, must go down in history as one of those fateful warnings uttered by a statesman to a full house that, having ears to hear, refused to listen.

Warning against the futility of force to make the Americans heel, Burke argued that the "temper and character" of the Americans rendered strong-arm tactics useless. Let's listen to one of the last pleas Burke made for reconciliation, in Parliament, a month before British soldiers fired on the militia at Lexington:

> In this character of the Americans, a love of freedom is the predominating feature which marks and distinguishes the whole; and as an ardent is always a jealous affection, your colonies become suspicious, restive and untractable, whenever they see the least attempt to wrest from them by force or shuffle from them by chicane, what they think the only advantage worth living for.
>
> This fierce spirit of liberty is stronger in the English colonies probably than in any other people of the earth; and this from a great variety of powerful causes, which to understand the true temper of their minds, and the direction which this spirit takes, it will not be amiss to lay open somewhat more largely.
>
> First, the people of the colonies are descendants of English-men. England, sir, is a nation which still I hope respects, and formerly adored, her freedom. The colonists emigrated from you, when this part of your character was the predominant; and they took this bias and direction the moment they parted from your hands. They are therefore not only devoted to liberty, but to liberty according to English ideas, and on English principles. . . .
>
> Religion, always a principle of energy in this new people is in no way worn out or impaired; and their mode of professing it is also one main cause of this free spirit. The people are

Protestants; and of that kind which is the most adverse to all implicit submission of mind and opinion. This is a persuasion not only favorable to liberty, but built upon it.

I do not think, sir, that the reason of this averseness in the dissenting churches, from all that looks like absolute government, is so much to be sought in their religious tenets as in their history. Every one knows that the Roman Catholic religion is at least coeval with most of the government where it prevails; that it has generally gone hand in hand with them, and receives great favor and every kind of support from authority.

The Church of England too was formed from her cradle under the nursing care of regular government. But the dissenting interests have sprung up in direct opposition to all the ordinary powers of the world; and could justify that opposition only on a strong claim to natural liberty. Their very existence depended on the powerful and unremitted assertion of that claim.

All Protestantism, even the most cold and passive, is a sort of dissent. But the religion most prevalent in our northern colonies is a refinement on the principles of resistance; it is the dissidence of dissent and the Protestantism of the Protestant religion.[1]

In the last half of the eighteenth century the Church of England became aware that the colonies—peopled by descendants of those forced to flee England—was a fertile land for spiritual imperialism. But before any kind of ecclesiastical expansion could take place, Puritanism, that "Protestantism of the Protestant religion" to which Burke referred, would have to be toppled.

The church obviously could be more effective if an Anglican episcopate were established in New England. Every colonial candidate for ordination in the Anglican church had to make a 6,000-mile trip in a sailing vessel in order to "take orders." Drownings were not uncommon among those making the arduous journey. As Boston radical Jonathan Mayhew taunted, "few were moved by the Holy Ghost" to face the danger or the expense.[2]

"As a result," Claude H. Van Tyne writes, "the Anglican clergy in America were often such as had failed in England, shepherds to whom their flocks looked up and were not fed. Though there were differences of opinion it was believed that they drank harder than they prayed, were more faithful to card-playing than to their congregations, and were better connoisseurs of fighting cocks than of souls."[3]

The missionary arm of the Church of England—the Society for the Propagation of the Gospel in Foreign Parts—and the Bishop of London intermittently pressed for a plan to plant Anglican bishops in America.

If there was one issue Americans were united on in the two decades before the Revolution, it was their hatred of Anglican bishops. They scorned the "pomp, grandeur, luxury and regalia of an American Lambeth [Lambeth Palace, in England, was the official residence of the Archbishop of Canterbury]."[4] Puritan preachers lambasted "imperious bishops who love to lord it over God's heritage."[5]

Those not especially concerned with the religious implications of native bishops were appealed to with the political argument that only the British Parliament could approve the establishment of an episcopacy in America. Parliament could both interfere with internal religious issues and impose internal taxes.

Almost forty years after the Revolution, an aging John Adams, looking out upon the diverse religious landscape of America, which included Anglican bishops, Methodist bishops, and Jesuits, exclaimed in a letter: "Who will believe that the apprehension of the Episcopacy contributed fifty years ago, as much as any other cause, to arouse the attention not only of the inquiring mind, but of the common people, and urge them to close thinking on the Constitutional authority of Parliament over the Colonies?

"There is no power or pretended power, less than Parliament, that can create bishops in America," Adams continued, warning that "close thinking" Americans feared permitting bishops to land in America would open a whole Pandora's box of ecclesiastical authority. "But if Parliament can erect dioceses and appoint bishops, they may introduce the whole hierarchy, establish tithes, forbid marriages and funerals, establish religions, forbid dissenters, make schism heresy, impose penalties extending to life and limb as well as to liberty and property."[6]

In Parliament Lord Chatham summarized the American attitude toward Anglican church leaders with his pithy comment: "Divided as they are into a thousand forms of polity and religion, there is one point in which they all agree: they equally detest the pageantry of a king and the supercilious hypocrisy of a bishop."[7]

The intermingling of civil and religious issues, as Carl Bridenbaugh points out, reached the flash point in the passage of the Stamp Act on March 22, 1765. Americans were outraged. A firestorm of protest swept across the colonies.

The national revulsion against proponents of the measure was not diminished by the news from England that nine bishops—bishops served in the House of Lords—were among the king's ministers who "were for carrying Fire and Sword to America, with this Argument, that since you snarle and begin to shew your teeth, they ought to be knocked out before you are able to bite."[8]

Bridenbaugh argues that "the colonial [Anglican] clergy

formed the core of the American Tories" who coalesced into a political movement with the passage of the Stamp Act.[9] Even those Tory ministers who saw the Stamp Act as bad politics urged their parishioners to remain loyal to the crown and comply with the law.

The dissenting clergy, with their fingers on the public pulse, denounced the act in righteous tones. Adams again attests to the influence of the patriotic clergy who arouses the "unconquerable rage of the People."[10] The polemical sermons and widespread opposition made political leaders more daring and bolder as they pushed for revocation of the Stamp Act. The importance the politicians placed on having ministers hew to the Whig party line is reflected in a resolution passed at a public meeting in New London, Connecticut, in December of 1765: "It is *presumed* no Person will publicly, in the Pulpit, or otherwise, inculcate the doctrine of passive Obedience, or any other doctrine to quiet the Minds of the People, in a tame submission to an unjust Imposition."[11]

The clergy, however, needed no prodding from public meetings. They hated the Stamp Act with a perfect hatred—after all, they could read. And the handwriting in the Stamp Act caused their gore to rise. The new law, intended to go into effect in November of 1765, called for the affixing of stamps on all documents, including copies of wills, "in *ecclesiastical* matters in any court of probate, court of the ordinary, or other court exercising *ecclesiastical* jurisdiction within said colonies. . . ."[12]

The Act clearly implied the establishment of church courts—and no Dissenting minister would permit that Trojan horse to be stabled in the colonies.

If the oppressive Stamp Act stayed on the books, the Dissenting clergy thundered, how much longer would it be before tax-burdened Americans would have to pay tithes to support luxury-loving Anglican clergy, pass religious tests to prove their Episcopal views in order to hold public office, and submit to laws interpreted by ecclesiastical courts? Freedom-intoxicated colonials shuddered at the prospect.

The dissenting clergy, an observer wrote, "were the chief Instruments in promoting and spiriting up the people to the Pitch of Madness, Tumult and Disaffection which so generally prevailed . . . during the Stamp Act Times."[13] Mob violence became common in the streets of Boston. Authority holders were intimidated. One mob leader, Ebenezer Mackintosh, loved to parade through the streets of Boston with two hundred men in double file. Mackintosh made it a point to march by the State House, where the General Assembly was in session, to impress the legislators that they would be held accountable for their actions. The Stamp Act rioter supposedly could squelch a whisper in the ranks merely by lifting a finger!

Resistance to the Stamp Act—it was wisely repealed on March 18, 1766, thereby averting "an open and armed rebellion"—was only the tip of the American opposition iceberg. A real "fear of conspiracy" on the part of the British ministry to deprive Americans of their rights as English subjects had become a national bugaboo in the colonies. Members of the British government were seen as evildoers plotting against loyal subjects.

However, up to the time of the meeting of the First Continental Congress, King George III was still held in high repute in the colonies. Protesters blamed the king's advisors and Parliament as being responsible for passing laws that eroded American freedoms. But as C. S. Lewis wrote in another context: "In the earlier history of every rebellion there is a stage at which you do not yet attack the King in person. You say, 'The King is all right. It is his Ministers who are wrong. They misrepresent him and corrupt all his plans—

which, I'm sure, are good plans if only the Ministers would let them take effect.' And the first victory consists in beheading a few Ministers: only at a later stage do you go on and behead the King himself."[14] In the Declaration of Independence, Thomas Jefferson turned "Good King George" into a tyrant running amok.

Bernard Bailyn believes the "fear of conspiracy" wrought a transformation in the American mind. From one of trust and affection for England as the protector of basic human rights, the American attitude slowly changed. England became increasingly regarded with suspicion as the center of conspiracy, and Englishmen were seen as intent on depriving the colonists of their God-given rights. "They saw about them, with increasing clarity, not merely mistaken, or even evil, policies violating the principles upon which freedom rested, but what appeared to be evidence of nothing less than a deliberate assault launched surreptitiously by plotters against liberty in both England and America." Bailyn pushes his conspiracy theory so far as to contend that "it was this above all else that in the end propelled them into the Revolution."[15]

The dissenting clergy and their congregations were suspicious of anything that smacked of the expansion of the Episcopal Church. That "sinister Episcopalian influence" always lurked near the surface in the minds of Nonconformists.

The Church of England came to America with the first ship of settlers who founded Jamestown, Virginia, in 1607. James I had inserted in the charter of Virginia that "the true word and service to God" was to be "preached, planted and used" in the new colony "according to the doctrine, rites and religion now professed and established within our realm of England." The law of the land demanded that everyone attend Episcopal services. The Old Dominion continued to be the stronghold of the Anglican Church in the colonies.

The Church of England also was the official faith in Georgia, the Carolinas, Maryland, and New York City at the outbreak of the Revolution. Nonconformists in New England and the Middle Colonies continually feared that the Anglican Church, an arm of the state, worked in concert with the crown to make all British subjects members of the Church of England. The church, in turn, returned the favor by preaching obedience and submission to the crown.

The Anglican Church in the colonies, minus its bishops, was seriously handicapped. Only bishops could confirm new converts and ordain clergy to fill the ranks to serve new churches. Missionaries for the Society for the Propagation of the Gospel in Foreign Parts, most of whom were Oxford graduates, acted as enemy agents behind the lines to proselytize Nonconformists and to promise an American episcopacy.

The perceptive Jonathan Mayhew, who prided himself on spotting a plot while it was still only the size of a man's hand, wrote to an influential friend on April 16, 1762: "We are apprehensive, sir, that there is a scheme forming for sending a bishop into these parts; and that our governor, Mr. Bernard, a true churchman [Anglican], is deep in the plot. This gives us a good deal of uneasiness, as we think it will be of bad consequences."[16]

Critics of the society accused the Anglican missionaries of deception. The outward pose that the missionaries came to America to evangelize the pagan Indians and Negroes concealed their real purpose. The society missions, Mayhew carped, have "all the appearances of entering wedges . . . carrying on the crusade, or spiritual siege of our churches, with the hope that they will one day submit to an episcopal

sovereign."[17] Even Bailyn appears to have accepted the view
that the Anglican missionaries were a group of dissemblers
whose "true goal was manifestly revealed when it established
missions in places like Cambridge, Massachusetts, which had
not had a Resident Indian since the seventeenth century and
was well equipped with 'orthodox' preachers."[18]

Actually, the Anglican missionaries were carrying out the
spirit as well as the letter of their charter by establishing
missions in places like Cambridge. The society charter,
granted by King William III, in 1701, explicitly stated the
goals of the organization:

> Whereas we are credibly informed, That in many of our
> Plantations, Colonies and Factories beyond the seas, belong-
> ing to our Kingdom of England, the Provisions for ministers
> [i.e., Anglican] is very mean; and many others . . . are wholly
> destitute and unprovided of a maintenance of ministers and
> the public worship of God [i.e., Anglican service]; and for lack
> of support and maintenance for such, many of our loving
> subjects do want the administration of God's Word and
> Sacraments. . . .[19]

The primary thrust of the society was to promote the
Church of England in "foreign parts," with the conversion of
Indians and Negroes a second but separate goal.

Religion and politics, however, were closely intertwined in
the attempt of the Church of England to plant resident
bishops in America. The ineptness of the Anglican Church in
landing a bishop in America was surpassed only by the
blunders of the king's men in creating and implementing
colonial policies. British clergy and politicians alike contributed immensely to American independence. The basically
religious question of an Anglican episcopate in America was

shrewdly politicized by the militants opposing British policies. Americans became convinced that permitting Anglican bishops to land on American soil would result in spiritual bondage as surely as the unopposed presence of British Redcoats in Boston presaged political tyranny for all Americans.

Anglican evangelist George Whitefield, whose powerful, theatrical preaching made him one of the most popular public figures in colonial America, reinforced the widely shared view that the push to send bishops to the colonies opened the door to tyranny. His warning, imparted in private to two ministers in Portsmouth in April of 1764, had an ominous ring: "I cannot in conscience leave the town without acquainting you with a secret. My heart bleeds for America. O poor New England! There is a deep laid plot against both your civil and religious liberties, and they will be lost. Your golden days are at an end. You have nothing but trouble before you. My information comes from the best authority in Great Britain."[20]

Whitefield's "secret" was made public by Dr. Samuel Langdon, who repeated it in a sermon before the New Hampshire Convention. It contained the usual threats of "general taxation of the colonies, alterations of the chartered governments, the introduction of bishops, tithes for the support of the clergy, and public offices for Episcopalians only."[21]

Opposition to Anglican bishops was not confined to New England, where Congregationalism was in effect established. The wealthy planters of Virginia, who controlled the Episcopal Church in the Old Dominion, resented resident bishops as an interference in their religious affairs. A few of the Virginia clergy favored creating an American bishopric, but critics impugned their motives, saying the pro-bishop clergy were interested in a "pair of lawn sleeves" for themselves.

Proponents of an episcopate in America recognized that

unless the New England Anglicans could rally the support of the southern colonies, where the church was established by law—but not in spirit—they could never pull off their scheme of bringing a bishop to the spiritually benighted plantations.

The lukewarmness of even the Episcopal clergy in Virginia toward a bishop was reflected in an abortive attempt in May of 1771 for a convention of Virginia clergy to discuss "the Expediency of an Application to proper Authority for an American Episcopate." The Church of England in Virginia listed more than one hundred clergymen on her roster. Only eleven responded to the conference call, and four of those voted against petitioning for a bishop!

Why were Episcopal clergy opposed to the establishment of an episcopate? In simple terms, self-interests. Like most human beings, they did not look forward to having to answer to a superior. Besides, they were making a good living, thank you, with the help of local vestrymen. Why change a good thing?

Carl Bridenbaugh points out that the Episcopal laity in Virginia "enjoyed through their vestries a virtually congregational form of church polity, which neither they nor the majority of any parish clergy had any remote desire to change. Republicanism in religion existed in all of the colonies, not just in New England."[22]

Americans would no more tolerate a church imposed on them from abroad than they would a monarchial form of government. The "leveling" concept of all men having been created equal did not mesh well with a hierarchical church. The colonial bent was in a different direction.

The forces threatening to sever Great Britain from her colonies received a boost with the reprint in August of 1770 of "A Plan for the Better Government of British America," written in 1769. The two general principles enunciated in the plan, printed in *Lloyd's Evening Post*, reflected fully how out of touch the British were with their colonies: "That inequality of rank and fortune is not only requisite for the support of every government, but essentially necessary to the interests and the best existence of society." Even more of a bombshell: "That an established religion, or one prevailing sect, or mode of religion, is absolutely needful to the well-being and permanency of every government."[23]

The conclusion based on those two general propositions supplied the Whig war hawks with an abundance of ammunition in their ideological struggle. The author asserted "that a political inequality, and proper established religion, ought to take place in America without delay, which last can only be effected by the appointment of Bishops, a regular performance of the rites of the Church of England, and a due administration of its ordinances."

Even two hundred years removed from the scene, one can almost feel the raising of the colonists' republican hackles by the arrogance of the British. The plan's author added insult to injury by proposing that the first bishop be seated in Boston, the Vatican of Puritanism! All thirteen colonies then would be divided into three dioceses, and King George III would thus be crowned "King of North America and the Isles." The plan succeeded only in driving another wedge between Great Britain and her colonies. Americans had been practicing local control of church and civil government for one hundred fifty years. These pious dissenters would never abdicate those rights without a fight—as the British, to their dismay, learned too late.

How much impact did the threat of settling bishops in America have in pushing the two nations into war? Scholars disagree on that question. Dr. Arthur Lyon Cross, whose *The Anglican Episcopate and the American Colonies*, published in

1902, still stands as an important work, maintained that the politically "strained relations" between England and her colonies acerbated the religious controversy, rather than the other way around. His conclusion was:

> Undoubtedly, there is something to be said in favor of the argument that the attempt to introduce bishops, and the opposition thereby excited, formed one of the causes of the Revolution. There can be no doubt that the opposition to bishops was based mainly on political grounds; this fact is indicated by the absence of any resistance to the establishment of an episcopate after the Revolution. Moreover, fear and hatred of the Church of England and all its appendages were existent in the colonies from their first foundation; and the fact that the majority of the colonists professed a religion hostile, or at least alien, to the Anglican establishment offered good ground for nourishing the seeds of political discontent. But, admitting all this, it must be apparent to one who has followed carefully the course of events, religious and political, during the eighteenth century, that the strained relations which heralded the approach of the War of Independence strengthened the opposition to the episcopacy, rather than religious differences were a prime moving cause of political alienation.[24]

Writing twenty years later, Claude H. Van Tyne found it "hard to agree with this last opinion [of Cross's] unless it is limited solely to the Anglican Episcopate controversy, and does not include other religious differences, cumulative in effect and creating a general spirit of discontent. Different issues were at different periods uppermost in men's minds, and, though they might at times seem most concerned with economic grievances, the religious one was deep and abiding."[25]

But Carl Bridenbaugh, in his more recent work, again

accents the difficulty the modern mind has in recovering "imaginatively a real understanding of the enormous effect of this controversy on the opinions and feelings of a pious, dissenting people grown accustomed to ecclesiastical self-government and currently engaged in a struggle to protect their liberties in the civil sphere. The agitation over an American episcopate reached its peak by 1770 and the public had almost grown frenzied in the course of it. . . .

"Eight years before Lexington, when the ministers learned that 'the Bishops are coming,' they wrote and spread the alarm all over the colonies. The people were roused and kept the watch."[26]

It is true, as Dr. Cross argued, that resistance to an Anglican episcopate ceased after the War of Independence was won. But the episcopate had been transformed by the war. Episcopal bishops now would no longer be "foreign agents," introduced from abroad, but would be homegrown products presiding over the Protestant Episcopal Church of America. An independent, American church had the right to choose its own structure. If the members wanted bishops in "lawn sleeves," then so be it. The important thing was that the Episcopalians, like the Congregationalists in New England and the Presbyterians in the Middle Colonies, now had home rule. That's what the shouting was all about in the first place.

Another wind of change had already swept across the colonies—one not all the might of kings or prelates could halt.

NINE

Awakening

The Great Awakening swept across the thirteen colonies with the force of a spiritual tornado, touching down on crowded cities and remote villages, leaving behind ecstatic converts, bitter critics, and divided churches. Ironically, the revival that split churches united the colonies into a mass Jesus movement. "The goal of the revivalists was, as Samuel Finley phrased it, 'to make up a party for Jesus Christ.' "[1] Until Betsy Ross could get around to sewing the American flag, the colonists would rally around the Christian banner.

Alan Heimert argues that the Great Awakening divided American Protestantism into "two streams of thought— evangelical and rational." The Harvard historian challenges the traditional view that liberal ministers provided the theological underpinnings for the Revolution. In fact, Heimert contends, just the opposite is true. The liberals were "the most reluctant of rebels." The liberal clergy were basically conservative politically and socially. They wanted to preserve the status quo and preached against the egalitarian idea that all men are created equal.[2]

By the time the Great Awakening began to change the

spiritual landscape of colonial America, Puritanism on the Atlantic seaboard had developed a strong rationalistic streak. Slowly reason began to replace revelation. Puritan divines preached that God could be known as well through His works as through His Word. Religious fervor was beginning to cool.

The concept that God had entered into a covenant with the saints in the colonies also began to break down. The Half-Way Covenant, which lowered the requirements for church membership, failed to achieve its goal of adding more members. In fact, it had just the opposite effect. Religion had become formal and void of emotional content. As a result, interest in things of the spirit diminished. More and more emphasis was placed on morality and less and less attention given to life-changing personal conversion. The Age of the Enlightenment took its toll in the colonial churches.

Many settlers, living long distances from any church and seldom hearing a sermon or partaking of the sacraments, became indifferent and secularized. "Times were thus ripe for some new emphasis in religion as well as a new type of religious leadership to meet the peculiar situation which the American colonies presented."[3]

The "new emphasis" would be the "old Calvinism" the early Puritans preached when they flooded the New England plantations. Puritanism had always been caught in the tension between rationalism and piety. The seventeenth-century church fathers in Massachusetts had managed to keep the two in delicate balance. But subsequent generations emphasized the rationalistic dimension of the faith, draining it of its heartfelt convictions.

The Great Awakening did not begin with the formation of committees, cottage prayer meetings, intensive visitation, and media saturation. Rather, it was a spontaneous outpouring of the Spirit upon various churches in separate sections of the country. The rivulets of revival spread across the spiritually parched countryside, then merged into a mighty stream to sweep thousands into the Kingdom of God.

The nationwide revival was unusually effective because of its evangelical ecumenism. Its chief spokesman and most articulate defender was the brilliant Jonathan Edwards, a Congregationalist. Gilbert Tennent, a fearless Presbyterian preacher, spread the revival fires among the brethren in New Jersey. And George Whitefield, the silver-tongued Anglican evangelist, moved from colony to colony and across denominational lines to make a national movement out of the message of the new birth.

The Awakening is important to this study on the role of religion in the Revolution because, in the words of Heimert, "What the colonies had awakened to in 1740 was none other than independence and rebellion."[4] Strange as it may sound, the nationwide revival provided pre-Revolutionary America with a political ideology growing out of the radical religious movement. The shared religious experience inspired "a thrust toward American nationalism." As a result, "the uprising of the 1770s was not so much a result of reasoned thought as an emotional outburst similar to religious revival."[5]

As the revival spread, increased resistance came from the liberal clergy, who saw the egalitarian religious movement as a threat to their preferred position in colonial society. The emphasis upon the "new birth" bothered the old-line Puritan clergy. They believed one should derive his knowledge of God through an intellectual process and not take emotional shortcuts. The revivalists taught and testified that one could have a personal encounter with God in Christ through an act of faith in an instant. Thus the critics of the Great Awakening accused the evangelical Calvinists of being emotionally overcharged. The evangelicals countered that rational religion neither satisfied the yearning of the human heart nor produced salvation.

The Calvinist psychology asserted that "the New Birth carried with it a realization that man's true happiness was derived not merely from his dependence on God but from his interdependence with his fellowmen. In this idea, as expanded and enforced on the American mind in the decades after the Awakening, consisted the most enduring of Calvinism's contributions to American political thought and practice."[6] A nation of newborn men would form a more perfect union, in which God's will could be carried out. Edwards was convinced that "the latter-day glory [millennium] is probably to begin in America."[7] Charles Chauncy, leader of the liberals, rebuffed Edwards by quoting the Puritan patriarch Increase Mather, that it was "the Judgement of very Learned Men, that in the glorious Times promised to the Church on Earth, America will be Hell."[8]

The powerful preaching of Jonathan Edwards caused his converts to look at life differently. Edwards believed true "religious affections" brought about change in both the individual and society. The born-again believer carried out God's will with infinite joy. Redemption not only prepared one for heaven, it also made one a better citizen. Edwards had a burning vision of a transformed society crowning Christ as king and reveling in God's supreme law of love. The radical ideas of the revivalists later neatly dovetailed with the political ideology that shaped the American Revolution. As the architect of revivalist theology, Edwards is worthy of a closer look.

As a youth, Jonathan Edwards exhibited the traits that later would make him the intellectual leader of the Great Awakening.

Edwards showed early signs of being a mystic. As a young man he liked to walk in the meadows and woods of his father's farm and think God's thoughts after Him. His passion for prayer and meditation, however, never blunted his curiosity and delight in nature. He made a scientific study of spiders before entering Yale College when he was not yet thirteen. (He was valedictorian of his class of ten when he graduated— at the age of seventeen.)

At twenty-four, Edwards joined his grandfather, Solomon Stoddard, the "Protestant pope" of Northampton, Massachusetts, as assistant pastor. Stoddard died two years later, and the young Edwards moved up to become the pastor of the most important parish outside of Boston.

The tall, slender, solemn young minister was disturbed by what he saw taking place in his parish. He records that the young people of Northampton were "very much addicted to night walking and frequenting the tavern, and lewd practices wherein some by their example exceedingly corrupted others." He objected to the mixed gatherings "which they called frollics," but which often would last "the greater part of the night."[9] He believed the parents should shoulder much of the blame for the waywardness of their children because "indeed family government did too much fail in the town."

Edwards was a student at heart. He "spent thirteen hours daily in his study, preparing two sermons a week." One night, in nearby Enfield, Edwards preached a sermon called "Sinners in the Hands of an Angry God," which caused many in the congregation to fall on their knees and beg God for mercy. He delivered the sermon in even tones, while keeping his eyes on the bell rope hanging in the back of the church.

His words were like ramrods, driving the realities of eternity into the minds of his listeners.

Unfortunately, the subject matter and the reaction to the sermon caused Edwards to go into the history books as a fire-and-brimstone Puritan preacher who delighted in describing the terrors of hell.

The historian James Truslow Adams blames Edwards, saying he swung "New England back to the horrors of its Calvinism and preached a gorilla God of such fiendish deviltry as surpassed the bloodiest heathen Moloch."[10]

Sydney Ahlstrom balances the books on Edwards by noting that "there are fewer than a dozen imprecatory sermons among the more than a thousand for which manuscripts are extant."[11] But Edwards continues to be victimized by compilers of anthologies who select the Enfield sermon as "typical" of the mentality of eighteenth-century Calvinists.

Edwards was no pulpit-pounding, Bible-thumping, ranting preacher. "In the pulpit he was quiet, speaking without gesture, and in a voice not loud but distinct and penetrating. It was the content of his sermons, filled as they are with fire and life, combined with the remarkable personality and presence of the preacher"[12] that made his preaching so powerful.

The revival under Edwards, in Northampton, began on a cold December Sunday in 1734. It did not stem from a vivid word-picture of the torments of hell. Rather, the spiritual renaissance resulted from a series of closely reasoned sermons on justification by faith. The sermons were not prepared to press for "decisions for Christ." They were intended to throw a theological roadblock in the way of the advance of liberalism. Edwards feared that the rationalists were undermining the foundations of the faith once delivered by the saints who formed the Holy Commonwealth in Massachusetts.

The revival's impact could be seen as well as felt. Religion became the prime topic of conversation. The interest in spiritual matters was so keen that "other discourse than of the things of religion would scarcely be tolerated in any company."[13]

The Northampton revival passed the litmus test of the New Testament—love your enemies. "I never saw the Christian spirit in Love to Enemies so exemplified, in all my Life as I have seen it within this half-year," Edwards wrote to Benjamin Colman, pastor of Brattle Street Church in Boston.[14] Edwards's heart was filled to the bursting point as he wrote how the town seemed to be full of the presence of God. The revival increased his own church rolls by three hundred new members.

Edwards was a rationalistic mystic who espoused a restrained form of revivalism. He was willing to concede that one may be saved without some of the physical manifestations that became the hallmark of the revival. He even admitted that some of the more emotional outbursts could be demonic in origin. He was convinced, however, that the revival was genuine and that "we must throw by our Bible, and give up ye revealed religion, if this be not, in general, the work of God."[15]

Edwards knew from experience that conversion was not always a cataclysmic event. In his own "Personal Narrative" he gives this moving account of the gentleness of his New Birth:

> I walked abroad . . . in my father's pasture, for contemplation. And as I was walking there, and looking up on the sky and clouds, there came into my mind so sweet a sense of glorious majesty and grace of God, that I know not how to express. I seemed to see them both in sweet conjunction;

majesty and meekness joined together. . . . After this my
sense of divine things gradually increased, and became more
and more lively, and had more of that inward sweetness. The
appearance of every thing was altered; there seemed to be, as
it were, a calm, sweet cast, or appearance of divine glory, in
almost every thing. God's excellency, his wisdom, his purity
and love, seemed to appear in every thing; in the sun, moon,
and stars; . . . flowers, trees, in the water, and all nature.[16]

The Awakening became a storm center in the churches
after the first wave of revival hit. It divided the Congregationalists into New Lights (proponents) and Old Lights (opponents). The Presbyterian Church was split between the New
Sides, who favored the revival, and the Old Sides, who
opposed it.

Regeneration became the hallmark of a Christian in the
Great Awakening. Piety and prayers were emphasized. De-
votional books were in demand. Before the revival bottomed
out, between 20,000 and 50,000 persons would become
members of colonial congregations.

One of the leading rationalist ministers, the haughty
Charles Chauncy, of Boston's First Congregational Church,
looked with disdain on the eighteenth-century holy-rollers
who disrupted the order of staid Puritan churches.

Chauncy left us one of the more vivid descriptions of the
revival's impact: "Numbers of people continued the greater
part of the night in utmost disorder; they were groaning,
crying out, laughing, congratulating each other, which they
did by shaking hands and embraces (the latter was commonly
practiced by different sexes) and by the fifth night, there were
almost three hundred affected."[17] Obviously Chauncy would
never permit that kind of religious frenzy to invade his
church.

Chauncy explained how religion out of kilter could only lead to "disorders": "There is," he explained, "the religion of understanding and judgment, and will, as well as of the affections; and if little account is made of the former while great stress is laid upon the latter, it can't be but people should run into disorders."[18]

Edwards's defense of the Awakening is found in his "A Treatise Concerning Religious Affections," published in 1746. The work is, in Ahlstrom's words, "one of America's profoundest inquiries into the nature of religious experience."[19]

In his treatise, Edwards argues that "true religion, in great part, consists in holy affections."[20] *Affections*, in Edwards's lexicon, was that force, or motive, deeper than emotions and fleeting passions, that moves "a person from neutrality or mere assent and inclines his heart to possess or reject something." This love becomes the "fountain of all the affections."

Edwards, ever the "rationalist revivalist," knew some conversions stemmed more from overwrought emotions than they did from the Holy Spirit. But he also had seen with his own eyes in his own parish of Northampton how the work of the Holy Spirit had "made a glorious alteration in the town."[21]

Edwards became the undisputed leader among the Calvinist clergy concerned to combat the spread of the more appealing Arminianism. In contrast to rigid Calvinism, the Arminians believed each individual had the choice to accept or reject God's offer of salvation in Christ. Arminianism contended that man's free will was not usurped by God's sovereignty.

Arminianism was the official theology of the Church of England. But even some Puritan divines of the eighteenth century preached that man was capable of "willing his own salvation."

To the logical mind of Jonathan Edwards, Arminianism was more than theological error. It bordered on blasphemy, in that it placed man at the center of events, leaving God out on the edges as a kind of Great Tinkerer "who must have little else to do, but to mend broken links as well as he can."[22] Trying to justify the ways of God, who is all-knowing and all-powerful, is not an easy task. But few men were ever better prepared intellectually than Jonathan Edwards.

Using classical Greek categories, Edwards answered the Arminian argument that even an act of the will cannot take place "without a Cause." Edwards was willing to admit men had a will, but he was convinced that logic and Scripture demanded that God, to be God, had to determine all things. In his brilliant treatise, *The Freedom of the Will* (1754), Edwards argued that a person will respond only to what appeals most to his own nature or preconditioned likes and inclinations.

Edwards brilliant mind and amazing psychological insights carried the field for the evangelical Calvinists. His influence extended far beyond his life. He put his stamp on New England preaching, which shaped pulpit practices for another one hundred years, and the revival replaced the owning-the-covenant ceremony as the door to salvation.

Alan Heimert, who often sees more political content in Edwards's writing than do most other historians, asserts that *Some Thoughts Concerning the Present Revival of Religion in New England*, written by Edwards in 1742, "was in a profound sense the first national party platform in American history. Yet Edwards' thoughts seem totally divorced from all the topics of which partisan issues are presumably made."[23]

Heimert contends: "For Edwards' 'Thoughts,' like the Awakening he defended, was in a vital respect an American declaration of independence from Europe, and the revival impulse was one toward intercolonial union. . . . The Awakening shattered social assumptions inherited from the previous century and provided the American people with new commitments, political as well as ethical."[24]

Evangelicals always had an affinity toward "popular forms of government." As early as 1742—when the Awakening was at its height—a Connecticut Anglican warned that the "best of people in all denominations" feared that the revivalists would "shortly get the government into their hands and tyrannize over us."[25] The evangelical impulse seemed to fit easily into democratic molds of government.

Perry Miller, the modern-day authority on Puritan New England, makes the important point that up to the time of Edwards, neither the civil nor the religious leader had to account for his actions to the people. He believed his duties had been spelled out in the Bible, executed his office without any reference to the temporary passions of the people, and reported directly to God.

The "leveling" thrust of the Great Awakening abolished that privilege. The minister could no longer stand in his pulpit, insulated from the people, claiming a direct pipeline to God. The voice of the people was more and more being heard in the land. Jonathan Edwards was aware that this change had taken place.

Edwards did not consciously try to promote a social revolution or even inject ideas of democracy into the body politic. He was, as Miller emphasizes, "born to the purple, to ecclesiastical authority. Yet he was the man who hammered it home to the people that they had to speak up, or else they were lost."[26] In the American wilderness, "the leader had to get down amongst them, and bring them by actual participation into the experience that was no longer private and privileged, but social and communal."[27]

The Great Awakening, many of Edwards's followers fervently believed, was a prelude to the millennium. Although that promise failed to materialize, the revival did have wide social impact. It diluted the loyalty of converts, who were looking for a new king and a new kingdom. England became the enemy, not so much because of her imperial policies, but because she had become a rich, decadent, and sinful society. The boundaries of the City of God and the city of man were blurred. The kingdom to come in America would be none other than the Kingdom of God. But first the Redcoats would have to be removed.

The mind-set that later infused political and military acts with spiritual meaning was expressed by an ecstatic evangelical who prophesied that America would become *"Immanuel's* land, a Mountain of Holiness, a Habitation of Righteousness! The Lord's spiritual Empire of Love, Joy and Peace will flourish gloriously in this Western World!"[28] The Promised Land had been rediscovered. Religious rhetoric and symbolism would be applied indiscriminately to political and military actions. Ministers would make God over into their own image. The face He presented—as depicted by the patriotic clergy—on the eve of the American Revolution, bore a striking resemblance to that of Mars, the Roman god of war. The patriotic Puritan preachers would unknowingly raise an abomination in the land. They believed so fervently in the righteousness of their cause that they would overlook the fact they had fallen into the greatest sin of all—national self-righteousness.

Edwards, who towered over the spiritual landscape during the Great Awakening, was in serious trouble with his own congregation by 1748. Critics in his congregation had formed a unified front to oust him from the pulpit. He had made a number of unforgivable errors, and one involved pornography. Upon learning the young men of the town were taking an inordinate interest in a new book on midwifery, from the pulpit he had castigated the culprits for reading dirty books. This upset their parents, who never forgave their pastor.

Next Edwards made the mistake of throwing out his grandfather's permissive procedure of allowing children of unregenerate parents to take communion. His methodical search of Scripture convinced him this was contrary to New Testament principles. But the "Stoddardean Way" was a hallowed tradition in Northampton, not open to tampering.

Edwards further aroused the opposition by requiring candidates for church membership to make a short public confession—a tradition that went all the way back to Governor Winthrop and the Founding Fathers of Massachusetts. But the Northampton congregation saw it as a power grab on Edwards's part. They argued Edwards had exhumed an ancient practice to increase his personal power base. The authority to determine who was eligible for church membership and the concomitant blessing of owning the covenant put one in an enviable position in Puritan society.

Colonel John Stoddard, chief of the militia, had been Edwards's prime protector in the civil society. When Colonel Stoddard died, Edwards preached his funeral sermon. As in the case of so many similar incidents in history, the orator chose the solemn occasion to press his personal views on a topic of great importance—the function and meaning of authority.

As Perry Miller points out in his penetrating commentary, John Winthrop "had commenced the New England tradition by telling the people they had the liberty to do only that which is in itself good, just and honest; that their liberty was the proper end and object of authority thus defined; that the approbation of the people is no more than the machinery by which God calls certain people to the exercise of designated powers."[29] In the Puritan concept of democracy, the people had to be silent when the minister spoke. The minister may have been elected by the congregation, but once installed in office, his authority was not to be questioned. Hence congregationalism was in action "a silent democracy in the face of a speaking aristocracy."

Jonathan Edwards contended that rather than the office making the man, the man should make the office. A ruler must be one who has a "great ability for the management of public affairs." Today we would say Edwards was stating the obvious. But in his own time, Edwards's statement was revolutionary. He changed the definition of a ruler from one who was correct in his doctrine to one who has natural abilities. Public leaders must be men capable of discerning "those things wherein the *public welfare* or *calamity consists*, and the proper *means* to avoid the one and promote the other."[30] Experience is this dominant theme in the funeral eulogy devoted to defining authority.

"Is this the great Puritan revivalist? It is. And what is he saying, out of the revival? He is telling what in political terms the revival really meant: that the leader has the job of accommodating himself to the realities of human and, in any particular situation, of social, experience. No matter what he may have as an assured creed, as a dogma—no matter what he may be able to pronounce, in the terms of abstract theology, concerning predestination and original sin—as a public leader he must adapt himself to *public welfare and calamity*. He cannot trust himself to a priori rules of an eternal and uncircumstanced good, and honest."[31]

Among the so-called mourners—few of Edwards's enemies wept tears over Stoddard, knowing his death left Edwards open to attack—were wealthy merchants, unscrupulous land speculators, and businessmen of soft morality. It was almost as if Edwards were aware this was his last opportunity to denounce the commercial establishment of the Connecticut Valley. His language is sharp and colorful as he warns that a proper ruler is one who opposes those "of a narrow, private spirit that may be found in little tricks and intrigues to promote their private interests, [who] will shamefully defile their hands to gain a few pounds, are not ashamed to hit and bite others, grind the faces of the poor, and screw upon their neighbors; and will take advantage of their authority or commission to line their own pockets with what is fraudulently taken or withheld from others."[32]

Edwards may have been preaching his protector's funeral, but he was also digging his own grave. In two years he would be forced from his pulpit in Northampton and sent into what his critics must have thought as an exile at the Stockbridge Indian Mission on the edges of the frontier.

But his time at Stockbridge was his most productive. There he penned his theological treatises *The Freedom of the Will* and *The Great Christian Doctrine of Original Sin*, plus several other books.

Edwards's banishment won him more fame than did his ministry at Northampton. Still the acknowledged leader of the revival movement, he was asked in 1758 to become president of the College of New Jersey—better known now as Princeton. He accepted, but died a few weeks after his inauguration—a victim of smallpox inoculation.

In October of 1740, Jonathan Edwards had sat in one of his own pews, weeping along with his congregation as they listened to the spellbinding oratory of a young evangelist from

England—George Whitefield. The eloquent Anglican had charmed the Northampton congregation, just as he had been an instant hit in Boston a few months earlier. Whitefield could not touch the hem of Edwards's garment intellectually. But he would capture the hearts and imagination of the American public. By so doing, this citizen of England and son of the Anglican Church would help prepare the ground for a political revolution in the thirteen colonies.

Popularly and properly called the "marvel minister," George Whitefield was idolized by the masses. He had an amazing voice that could clearly be heard in the open. His oratory could even make the tight-fisted Benjamin Franklin empty his pockets. When he died, he was mourned by more Americans than were the slain of the Boston Massacre.

This Anglican priest had been barred from preaching in the Church of England because of his "enthusiasm." When the established church slammed the doors in his face, Whitefield began preaching outdoors, to the miners and common people. Thousands flocked to hear him, and his fame soon spread throughout England and across the Atlantic.

The Great Awakening in America—a nationwide revival— began in scattered sections of New England and New Jersey in the late 1730s and early 1740s. When Whitefield arrived in America, the separate rivers of revival converged and became a mighty torrent, sweeping across the country with the force of a tidal wave.

Whitefield's arrival in New England in 1740 was preceded by his reputation and made front-page copy in the Boston papers. The Anglican evangelist was only twenty-six years old when he stormed the spiritual ramparts of Boston.

Whitefield had the stage presence of a Shakespearean actor, with a clear and musical voice that could be projected an unbelievable distance. He was of a solemn countenance with a squint in one eye. He spoke without notes—a strange sight to New Englanders, accustomed to ministers who preached from thick manuscripts. He also peppered his sermons with anecdotes, another departure from the traditional Puritan preaching style.

Whitefield's presence in Boston created more commotion than would the dumping of tea in the harbor several years later. So many people crowded into one church that five persons were killed in the panic. After that, Whitefield preached outdoors, attracting as many as eight thousand at a time.

One astute observer of the preacher was the aging Deist Benjamin Franklin. Whitefield, a compassionate man, sponsored an orphanage in Georgia, and wherever he went, he pleaded for funds for it. Franklin believed there was a greater need for an orphanage in metropolitan Philadelphia than in the backwaters of sparsely settled Georgia.

"I silently resolved he [Whitefield] should get nothing from me," Franklin wrote later. "I had in my pocket a handful of copper money, three or four silver dollars, and five pistols in gold. As he proceeded I began to soften, and concluded to give the copper.

"Another stroke of his oratory determined me to give the silver; and he finished so admirable that I emptied my pockets wholly into the collector's dish, gold and all."[33]

One night, while Whitefield preached from the courthouse steps in Philadelphia, Franklin, ever the scientist, decided to find out how many persons could hear Whitefield at one time.

Franklin slowly worked his way backwards down Market Street, until he could no longer hear. He concluded thirty thousand people could hear him preach in an open-air meeting!

Whitefield, more than any other evangelist, was responsible for turning the Great Awakening into a nationwide revival. Traveling the colonies from Georgia to New England, he preached to multitudes along the way. For the first time, the colonies became involved in a unifying, mass movement. Ritual and tradition were swept aside. The new birth and experimental religion became the hallmark of the Awakening.

At times it seemed Whitefield went out of his way to rankle the rationalistic ministers of New England. He blasted Harvard and Yale as liberal-leaning institutions that had left their first love of preaching the pure gospel. He also held the rationalistic ministers in contempt: "I am persuaded," he said, "the generality of preachers talk of an unknown and an unfelt Christ. The reason why congregations have been so dead is because they had dead men preaching to them. How can dead men beget living children?"[34]

Spiritual renewal both in England and the continent followed the same pattern. The more educated classes embraced the "generalities of the eighteenth-century rationalism," while the "spiritual hunger of the lower classes" was satisfied by the revivals.

When Whitefield preached at Harvard, even those intellectual giants succumbed to the power of the Spirit, making decisions for Christ. Then as the clerical establishment attempted to clamp down on itinerant "enthusiastic" evangelists by barring them from the pulpits of their churches, the students demonstrated against the infringement of religious liberty.

Whitefield left Boston after his first whirlwind tour in 1740, and thirty thousand citizens gathered on the common to bid him farewell. But not all in the crowd were well-wishers. Many of the clergy, perhaps a bit envious, felt relieved that the popular preacher was leaving their town.

When Whitefield returned on his second tour of New England, he had become such a controversial figure that he was considered a troublemaker and spoiler. Both Harvard and Yale refused him permission to speak. But the common folk once again heard him gladly, flocking to the fields to hear him preach.

The rationalist clergy may have considered Whitefield outside the pale, but the students at Yale protested the official hostility the college leadership extended to Whitefield and other revivalists. "By 1753, President Thomas Clap had been converted to the revivalist cause," Ahlstrom states.

In 1764 Whitefield returned to New Haven, for his fourth American visit, and was invited to preach at the college chapel. Whitefield had mellowed in his attitude toward ministers of differing creeds, but his charisma was not diminished by age.

"So moved were the students that they urged President Clap to call the great preacher from the coach in which he was departing and persuaded him to give them another quarter hour of exhortation. By this time Yale and its graduates were assuming a role in the American Evangelical movement that they would not relinquish for over a century."[35]

Whitefield made five tours of New England—the last three in 1754, 1764, and 1770. During his various visits, he preached an unbelievable total of ten thousand sermons. He died in 1770, in Newburyport, Massachusetts, expending all his energy to the very last in a superhuman attempt to keep on preaching wherever the crowds gathered. He lies buried beneath the pulpit of the First South Presbyterian Church of Newburyport.

George Whitefield came to America to evangelize and not to raise the political consciousness of the colonists. One of the spin-offs, however, of the Awakening was a receptivity to change and a sense of unity among the converts scattered throughout the colonies. At least indirectly, Whitefield helped undermine the authority of early kings in America by preaching supreme loyalty to Christ the King.

While the firebrand Jonathan Mayhew preached political sermons in 1750, Jonathan Edwards cautioned his congregation in Northampton that the real issues of the day were spiritual, as reflected in the struggle between the rationalists and the evangelicals over the issue of whether "religious affections" were trustworthy.

The evangelicals eventually shifted gears, however, and around 1755 they were beginning to call for better public schools and lower taxes that were beginning to squeeze the poor "to support the corruption and luxury of the rich great." Several decades later, when the national debate on the issue of loyalty and political purpose began, the religious fervor of the evangelicals began to manifest itself in more secular ways.

As Sydney Ahlstrom observed, the Great Awakening wrought basic changes in colonial church life. Baptism and the Lord's Supper became symbols rather than means of grace. Conversion experience replaced infant baptism as the decisive experience in entering the Kingdom. The unquestioned right of the established church to levy taxes was called into question. Many of the converts left the Congregational churches to become Baptists. Awakening converts became less concerned with doctrine and more interested in fellowship with born-again believers. "Fellowship became not so much interdenominational as intercolonial."[36]

The Great Awakening helped blur sectarian distinctions. Before a Philadelphia audience, Whitefield emphasized his evangelical ecumenism in an imaginary conversation with the Old Testament patriarch Abraham:

"Father Abraham," he inquired, looking heavenward, "who have you in heaven? Any Episcopalians?"

"No."

"Any Presbyterians?"

"No."

"Any Baptists?"

"No."

"Any Methodists, Seceders, or Independents?"

"No, no!"

"Why who have you there?"

"We don't know those names here. All who are here are Christians."[37]

The story makes Whitefield sound more broad-minded than he actually was. True, he would preach in any church that would open its pulpit to him, but he would have no fellowship with those he considered "unconverted."

There were those who were convinced the Great Awakening would produce the Great Society. If they could clear the land of the British, the millennium would be on its way. Religious and political ideals increasingly blended as the American Revolution approached. The *union* in *communion* became increasingly emphasized. A nation founded on Christian beliefs geared up for a holy war.

Both rationalists and evangelicals supported the war against Great Britain. The rationalists were first to start beating the war drums in the churches, but when the evangelicals joined up, they exceeded the liberals in enthusiasm for the cause. The rationalists were ready to do battle to preserve their establishment. But to the evangelicals, the "sins of the soft

British society posed a threat to the saints in America and to the kingdom of God on earth." As a result, the revivalists had a view of society that was far more revolutionary than that proclaimed by the liberal clergy. As Richard Bashman wrote, "A psychological earthquake had reshaped the human landscape."[38]

Heimert argues that the evidence of history shows that the liberalizing in the eighteenth century was a "profoundly elitist conservative ideology" while evangelicalism posed a "democratic challenge to a standing order in colonial America."[39] Heimert may indeed be guilty of "unduly deprecating" (Sydney Ahlstrom's term) the role of the liberal clergy on the power elite in the colonies during the American Revolution.[40] Both evangelicals and rationalists undoubtedly contributed to the Whig cause of overthrowing the authority of the British crown in America, but each marched to a different drummer. Evangelicals may have had the greater impact because of their fervency and zeal. After all, they had the greater entrée with the common people—those who did the fighting.

TEN

A Righteous Rebellion

In July of 1775, Boston was a British garrison. On the clogged streets Redcoats jostled one another and loyalists who had fled to Boston for protection. The British Army already had clashed with the colonists twice and paid a terrible price. It had been driven back from Concord and Lexington. What started as an orderly retreat had ended in a rout. British troops, feared and respected by fighting men around the world, had thrown away their weapons and fled under the fierce fire and sniping of American provincials, who set upon them like angry hornets. When the English soldiers staggered back to the safety of the little hills above Charlestown, known as *Breed's* and *Bunker's,* they must have been surprised to learn they had only lost 73 men out of more than 2,000.

The second and more devastating engagement took place almost two months later on one of those two hills—Breed's that is, not Bunker's. Countering their enemy's move to occupy Dorchester Heights, the Americans had thrown up fortifications overnight—to the amazement of the British.

Fortifying Breed's Hill had been an American mistake to begin with. The green colonial troops, unskilled in military science, ignored the army dictum of taking the high ground, which would have put them on top of Bunker Hill. Breed's Hill was within firing distance of the guns of the Royal Navy in Boston harbor and the Boston battery. The British could have exploited the blunder by landing troops on Charlestown Neck—behind the dug-in Americans—cutting them off. But instead, the British responded with a bigger blunder, a frontal assault.

As the colonists watched regiments of the world's mightiest army, bayonets fixed and in flawless military formation, march toward them, they should have fired a few shots and then scattered. Some did not because second in command Israel Putnam threatened to shoot deserters. Instead they waited— and watched as the Redcoats came so close they could see the brass matchboxes the grenadiers wore on their chests.

What made other inexperienced American troops stay and fight rather than run? The bravest of soldiers feel fear, yet another force countered that emotion. At least one gray-haired farmer is reported to have prayed aloud his reason for refusing to run: "I thank thee, O Lord, for sparing me to fight this day. Blessed be the name of the Lord." Most of those men huddled behind the fortifications on Breed's Hill had been assured by their ministers they were fighting for a righteous cause. The British troops, they had been told, were minions of a decadent nation sullying the soil of free and virtuous people. These colonists, repressing the hot terror that threatened their faith and composure, would rather die in a holy cause than run like rabbits for safety.

The British soldiers were within fifteen paces of the American redoubt when the first American volley mowed down their front ranks. Bearskin caps and red coats crumpled to the ground. Dying men screamed and thrashed, spilling their life's blood on the grass of Breed's Hill. The shredded

British companies went back down the hill to regroup and came back up again and again before the carnage was over. The Americans finally were forced to abandon their "stronghold." But the British had achieved a victory that came perilously close to resembling defeat. Nearly half the attacking troops—1,054 out of 2,200—had been killed or wounded. The American casualty list showed 500 dead or wounded. Though they had not won, the Americans had proved to themselves and the world that they were worthy warriors. The punishment inflicted on the British at Breed's Hill created a caution in the English command that plagued their strategy to the end of the Revolution.

The upper house of the Great and General Court of Massachusetts, the colonial legislature, was called the council. Once a year, on election day, the lower house elected counselors, as called for in the colony's charter, to advise the royal governor. But the governor in 1775 was the commander in chief of British forces in North America—General Thomas Gage. The illegal Provincial Congress of Massachusetts succeeded the general court, when it was disbanded by Gage. In July of 1775, the Provincial Congress assembled at Watertown. The colonists were not permitted to elect counselors, nor did they have any desire to do so. But it was the anniversary day fixed by charter for the election. Even though the provincials were denied their charter right to elect counselors, they still met to do as many things as they normally did on election day. One of those things was to listen to a sermon.

The minister delivering the election day sermon always had been carefully selected. It was a prestigious assignment, because the sermon would be printed and distributed throughout the colony. Some were even read as far away as England. In 1775, the signal honor was awarded to the Reverend Samuel Langdon, president of Harvard College.

Only six weeks earlier, at Lexington and Concord, the "first blood" of the war had been shed, and the fierce battle at Breed's Hill had taken place only three weeks earlier. The British had begun to mobilize their massive military power to cut off the colonists before they entered into a full-scale war. Boston was the center of the rebellion and the focal point of British retaliation. Affairs of government had fallen into a political limbo. The Continental Congress would not move for an independent government for another year.

President Langdon, who also was a Congregational minister, chose for his text Isaiah 1:26 (italics added): "And I will restore thy judges as at the first, and thy *counsellors* as at the beginning." It was a master stroke in text selection.

In an attempt to purge the rebellious Massachusetts Bay constitution of "all its crudities," the British ministry had practically eviscerated the colony's charter. The governor's council could no longer be elected but was appointed by the crown. Justices of the peace were to be picked by the royal governor, and even juries were to be selected by the crown-appointed sheriff. The British then rubbed salt into the political wound by restricting town meetings—the backbone of local government in Massachusetts—to those times and places permitted in writing by the governor.

President Langdon, keenly sensitive to the emotions and feelings roiling the minds of his audience, keyed his talk to the current troubles.

"Shall we rejoice, my fathers and brethren," he began, "or shall we weep together on the return of this anniversary, which from the first settlement of this Colony has been sacred to liberty, to perpetuate the invaluable privilege of choosing from among ourselves wise men fearing God and hating covetousness, to be honorable counsellors, to constitute an

essential branch of that happy government which was established in the faith of the royal charters?"[1]

The learned speaker continued to cater to the prevailing
mood of his listeners by reminding them that in the past they
had always assembled in Boston, which the British now had
turned into "a garrison for the mercenary troops." The
Harvard president saw this as a sure sign that "British liberty
is about ready to expire." Keep in mind that the Americans
believed that they were fighting for British liberty, which they
believed to be languishing on the island of its birth.
Independence was a word that only a few hotheads like Sam
Adams used to agitate the wharf toughs and street brawlers.
Even Adams, in his cooler moments, could assert as late as
1774, "I wish for a permanent union with the mother country,
but only on terms of liberty and truth. No advantage that can
accrue to America from such a union, can compensate for the
loss of liberty."[2] But the events of Lexington, Concord, and
Breed's Hill had silenced all talk of accommodation.

The Provincial Congress undoubtedly agreed with President Langdon that the conflict was caused by the wrongheaded policies of the British ministry and not by the king
himself, and Samuel Langdon reflected such a belief when he
stated, "That ever-memorable day, the nineteenth of April, is
the date of an unhappy war begun by the *ministers* of the king
of Great Britain against his good *subjects* in this colony, and
implicitly against all other colonies."

President Langdon also made it clear he believed the
mother country was on the verge of going over the brink to
moral destruction. "In a general view of the present moral
state of Great Britain it may be said, 'There is no truth, no
mercy, nor knowledge of God in the land.' " He continued to
lambast the British—not for the way in which they had
unfairly taxed their colonies or even deprived them of their

basic rights under the charter, but because of the way they treated God's elect in New England. "They have made a mock of our solemn feasts, and every appearance of serious Christianity in this land. On this account, by way of contempt, they call us 'saints'; and that they themselves may keep at the greatest distance from this character, their mouths are full of horrid blasphemies, cursing and bitterness, and vent all rage of malice and barbarity."

Dr. Langdon knew the colonists also had been tainted by sin, but that, too, had been imported by the British. Some of his audience may have squirmed as he lashed out: "But, alas! have not the sins of America, and of New England in particular, had a hand in bringing down upon us the righteous judgment of heaven? Have we not made light of the gospel of salvation, and too much affected the cold, formal, fashionable religion of countries grown old in vice, and overspread with infidelity? Have we not, especially in the seaports, gone much too far into the pride and luxuries of life?"

The sulphurous jeremiad of a Puritan preacher was a familiar form of address in eighteenth-century New England. As God's Chosen People in the Promised Land, they knew their Old Testament well enough to be aware that their sins offended God more than those committed by less enlightened nations.

The preacher also recognized that a listing of sins of the people and a call to repentance, resulting in God's renewed favor, could serve to "stiffen the patriotic spine" of the people.

Dr. Langdon assured his distinguished audience of political leaders that if true religion were revived in the nation's civil affairs, the army, in business and the family, "we may hope for the direction and blessing of the most high."

The college president cited battlefield statistics to prove

there were practical advantages to having God on your side in a shooting match: "In the late action at Chelsea," Dr. Langdon reported, "when several hundred of our soldiery, the greater part open unto the fire of so many cannons, swivels, and muskets, from a battery advantageously situated—from two armed cutters, and many barges full of marines, and from ships of the line in the harbor—not one man on our side was killed, and but two or three wounded; when by the best intelligence, a great number were killed and wounded on the other side, and one of their cutters was taken and burnt, the other narrowly escaping with great damage.

"If God be for us, who can be against us?"

President Langdon was confident that "the Most High who regards these things will vindicate his own honor, and plead our righteous cause against such enemies to his government as well as to our enemies." It was of the utmost importance militarily that Americans repent of their sins and embrace holiness. For such was the sure path to victory.

"O may our camp be free from every accursed thing. May we be truly a holy people, and all our towns and cities of righteousness. Then the Lord will be our refuge and strength, a very present help in time of trouble, and we shall have no reason to be afraid, though thousands of our enemies set themselves against us round about, though all nature should be thrown into tumults and convulsions. . . . May the Lord hear us in the day of trouble, and the name of the God of Jacob defend us, send us help from his sanctuary, and strengthen us out of Zion." President Langdon had clearly enlisted God on the side of the Americans, and now there could be no question of the outcome.

Historian J. T. Headley, who canonized the patriotic clergy, refers to "the fact that the rebellion in New England rested on the pulpit."[3] That may be an overstatement, but it did indeed receive strong support from this source. The Puritan clergy helped preach and pray the colonies into war and then devoted considerable energy to justify the ways of the revolutionaries to men and God. Their sermons failed to recognize that the rebellious acts of the Americans may have helped contribute to the conflict.

The patriot-preachers became effective propagandists, promoting a revolution that admittedly was based on high ideals and noble principles worthy of sacrifice. It is highly questionable, however, that the Revolution was a righteous rebellion that could be biblically justified.

In their detailed study of America's spiritual heritage, the authors of *The Search for Christian America*, sharply criticize the colonial Christians for "prostituting the gospel."

"American Christians in the late twentieth century should be appalled at the way in which the Bible, and Christian categories generally were abused in these several ways in the Revolution," the authors assert. "During the emotional fervor of the war patriots invested their cause with the kind of honor that belongs to God alone.

"The revival's [Great Awakening] opponents and proponents both rejected the Puritan heritage. But neither side constructed visible, biblically based alternatives. Even more they failed to ask how Scripture could offer guidance for getting along in a mixed culture where no one of the parties arising from the Awakening could dictate 'biblical politics' for the whole. As a result the gospel was prostituted, the church was damaged, and finally, the spread of the Christian faith itself was hindered."[4]

Those are strong words and perhaps the points are too finely drawn. Trying to stake out a biblically defensible position in a shooting war is no easy feat. Sometimes we concede, as did our most theological president, Abraham

Lincoln, that wars are caused by sin and as sinners we have to take sides and get on with the shooting and then seek God's forgiveness.

ELEVEN

The Sword of the Lord

The wheel of history had made another revolution when the Reverend Samuel West of Dartmouth preached his election day sermon on May 29, 1776. Boston now was back in the hands of the rebels, and General George Washington commanded the newly created American army. The Provincial Congress of Massachusetts had dissolved by its own act, on July 19, 1775, and reconvened the same day as the Honorable Council and Honorable House of Representatives. Local government was in a fluid state as it awaited the birth of a national government.

On May 16, 1775, a month after the shooting at Lexington and Concord, the Provincial Congress had informed the Continental Congress sitting in Philadelphia that the occupation of Boston by the British and the recent battles had placed the colony in a political limbo. The Great and General Court, which ruled in concert with the royal governor, no longer existed. The legislators had declined "to assume the reins of civil government without the advice and consent" of their sister colonies.

The letter explained that the besieged Massachusetts men

refused to set up a civil government because "the question equally affected our sister colonies and us." In other words, if the British could throw up a blockade around Boston, what would prevent them from doing the same to New York or Charleston? Then the letter closed with this political bombshell: "We hope you will favor us with your most explicit advice respecting the taking up and exercising the powers of civil government. . . . As the sword should, in all free states, be subservient to civil powers. . . . We beg leave to suggest to your consideration the propriety of *your* taking the regulation and general direction of the army."[1]

The message was clear: The Massachusetts congress was asking the Continental Congress to adopt the New England Army, thereby transforming it into an American army, and to set up a new civil government for all thirteen colonies.

The Continental Congress cautiously advised Massachusetts to "conform as near as may be to the spirit and substance of the charter" and to elect an assembly that would serve as a caretaker government "until a governor of his majesty's appointment would consent to govern the colony according to its charter."[2] The mood of the Congress in 1775 was reconciliation, not separation.

On June 16, 1775, exactly a month to the day after the Massachusetts letter had been received, the Continental Congress, under the exhortation of John Adams, established a "Grand American Army," an eloquent title for untrained militia. It fell to John Hancock, who had an inordinate desire to lead the American Army, to inform "George Washington, Esq., of the unanimous choice in choosing him to be General and Commander-in-Chief of the forces raised and to be raised in defense of American Liberty. The Congress hopes the gentleman will accept."[3]

King George III reached the end of his patience with the

upstart colonies on August 23, 1775, declaring that the American colonies were in "rebellion." He laid out his plans to Parliament for quelling the uprising. On December 22 a bill was passed interdicting all trade with the thirteen colonies. Open season was declared on all American ships and their cargo.

The Americans in the meantime had obtained fifty-nine pieces of artillery from Ethan Allen's attack on Fort Ticonderoga, transported them over the snow by ox cart, and positioned them on Dorchester Heights above Boston. General William Howe, who had succeeded General Gage, saw his position was untenable. Loading his troops and hundreds of Tory families (who had fled to Boston to escape the wrath of the rebels) onto his transports, he set sail for Halifax. On March 18, 1776, General Washington quietly entered Boston under a new flag—thirteen red and white stripes with the Union Jack in the canton. It was the beginning of the end for British rule in the colonies.

The Massachusetts Honorable Council and Honorable House of Representatives convened in May, 1776, in its old Town House, now usually referred to as the State House. The sermon would be given by the Reverend Samuel West in the "old brick meeting-house" nearby, on the site dedicated to the worship of God since 1640.

The Reverend Mr. West of Dartmouth was an old hand at expounding the rights of the colonies and attacking the wrongs of the British government in pulpit and press. West, a Harvard graduate, believed that reason and God dictated that the colonies should be free and independent.

His sermon, preached about five weeks before the Continental Congress adopted the Declaration of Independence, combined Lockean theory, eighteenth-century rationalism, and Puritan religious philosophy. In many points, it duplicates

Jonathan Mayhew's sermon of 1750. But unlike Mayhew, West preached in the midst of war. His theories were about to be put to the test. A long, carefully developed sermon, it required, in the words of John Adams, "close reasoning" by its hearers. The terminology was more rationalistic than Christian. For instance, West equated the voice of reason with the voice of God. He believed reason and Scripture never contradict each other. After all, how could the God of Reason contradict Himself in His inspired Word? Reason and Scripture always harmonized in the minds of the rationalistic Puritans.

West's text for his election sermon was Titus 3:1. "Put them in mind to be subject to principalities and powers, to obey magistrates, to be ready to every good work."

The Puritan rationalist was a realist. To West the human condition obviously required government for the safety and peace of all citizens. This was a necessity imposed by "our being in a fallen and degenerate state." (Even liberal Puritans believed in original sin.) God ordained government, and it was incumbent upon Christian citizens to obey those "good" rulers under whom Providence placed them. Civil obedience was not only a social requirement but a religious duty—up to a point, of course.

"I shall consider the nature and design of civil government," West began, "and shall show that the same principles which oblige us to submit to government do equally oblige us to resist tyranny. . . . I shall then apply the present discourse to the grand controversy that at this day subsists between Great Britain and the American colonies."[4]

The minister used a basic Lockean principle as the hinge of his argument—the source of legitimate authority. "It is necessary to derive civil government from its original, in order to which we must consider what 'state all men are naturally in, and that is (as Mr. Locke observes) a state of perfect freedom to order all their actions, and dispose of their possessions and persons as they think fit, within the bounds of the law of nature, without asking leave or depending upon the will of any man.' ' "

West emphasized that a state of nature does not give man the freedom to do what is right in his own eyes, "for a state of nature is properly a state of law and government."

Government comes from the hand of God, but man is free to choose the kind of government he wants to live under. All rulers, from the lowest magistrate to the king, hold office at the will of the people. Civil rulers are of human creation. "Consequently, the authority of a tyrant is of itself null and void." No person can "lawfully" enter into tyranny.

The speaker embraced the principle of majority rule. Obviously, laws can't be passed to please everyone. The minority may protest through legal means, but unless forced to break a divine law, the minority should submit to the majority.

West argued that first-century Christians never mounted a revolution against pagan rulers because there were so few Christians, it would have been futile to revolt. In other words, if you can't pull off a revolution, don't start one.

At this point in his sermon, West leaned more on Locke than on the Lord. He listed the criteria that must be met "when a people may claim a right of forming themselves into a body politic."

The first principle laid down by West in support of revolution was that the only binding laws are those made by the citizens themselves or their representatives. Representation and legislation are inseparable. Americans lived too far from London to be represented at Parliament, thus even "nature itself points to the necessity of their assuming to themselves the powers of legislation."

Oppression contributes to revolution. If wrongs cannot be redressed, then the colonists should "renounce all submission to the government that has oppressed them and set up an independent state of their own."

The Puritan preacher flops his argument to show that the same scriptural and rationalistic reasons that support good government undermine unlawful government: "I proceed, in the next place to show that the same principles that oblige us to submit to civil government do also equally oblige us, where we have power and ability, to resist and oppose tyranny; *and that where tyranny begins government ends*. For, if magistrates have no authority but what they derive from the people; if they are of properly human creation; if the whole end and design of their institution is to promote the general good, and to secure to men their just rights, it will follow, that when they act contrary to the end and design of their creation they cease being magistrates, and the people which gave them the authority have the right to take it from them again."

The wolves from Oxford who came over to America in the sheep's clothing of Anglican missionaries preached unlimited submission and obedience to the crown. "That kind of devotion is due only God. He alone has an uncontrollable sovereignty over us."

West did not attempt to delineate scriptural standards that determined when a tyrant should be deposed. He believed the public should make that decision. "Great regard ought always be paid to the judgment of the public."

Having argued from reason and natural law, in the third section of his lengthy lecture the minister relied more on Scripture.

West's application of Scripture followed the pattern set by

Jonathan Mayhew. Mayhew's real argument, however, was with English bishops not English kings. Not so with West; the British ministers had become the villains by 1776.

The clergyman explained the true meaning of Romans 13—the same passage Mayhew used to fire his "morning gun of the revolution." The passage begins: "Let every soul be subject unto the higher powers. For there is no power but of God: The powers that be are ordained of God. Whosoever therefore resisteth the power, resisteth the ordinance of God. . . ."

West echoed Mayhew—did he lift his arguments from Mayhew's widely read sermon?—by emphasizing parts of the passage that warn "rulers are not a terror to good works, but to the evil. . . . For he is the minister of God to thee for good. . ." (vv. 3, 4).

"It follows by undeniable consequence, that when they [rulers] become the pests of human society, when they promote and encourage evildoers and become a terror to good works, then they cease being the ordinance of God . . . and it is so far from being a crime to resist them that in many cases it may be highly criminal in the sight of Heaven to refuse resisting and opposing them to the utmost of our power."

West concluded by stating he had shown the colonists should resist the British while submitting to "our lawful magistrates"—meaning the Massachusetts Council and House of Representatives. He recognized there is a fine line to walk during a revolution to keep from slipping into anarchy. He boasted that Massachusetts was a shining example of how natural law works. When the colony's charter was vacated and the courts and legislative bodies were in limbo at the outbreak of the Revolution, the people still acted civilly. "That is a plain proof that they, having not the civil law to regulate themselves by, became a law unto themselves; and by their conduct have shown that they were regulated by the law of God written in their hearts. That is the Lord's doing, and it ought to be marvelous in our eyes." Locke and the Lord once again had triumphed in the holy Commonwealth.

The pastor-patriot turned from theory to the specific sins of the British, smiting them with righteous wrath. The king and Parliament had gone beyond depriving the colonists of their rights as Englishmen. The British had committed the unspeakable sin of trying to deprive the colonists of their rights to the good things of this present life to which they were entitled as Christians.

In the grand tradition of his forebears in the Puritan pulpit, West made resistance—and ultimately independence—a holy cause. "Our cause is so just and good that nothing can prevent our success but only our sins."

The Puritan-patriot, however, knew that facing sin head-on was the best way to prepare Christian soldiers for battle. Repentance leads to restoration and rearmament, moral and physical. Certainly the God of the thirteen colonies would not permit "liberty and true religion to be banished from off the face of the earth. But do we not find that both religion and liberty seem to be expiring and gasping for life in the other continent,—where, then, can they find a harbor or place of refuge but in this?"

West removed any doubt that the colonies should attempt to work things out with the British. Besides, he asked, had not England herself already treated the colonies as if they were independent?

"But when war is declared against a whole community without distinction, and the property of each party is declared to be seizable, this, if anything can be, is treating us as an independent state. Now, if they are pleased to consider us as in a state of independency, who can object against our considering ourselves so too?"

West's sermon is not important because it broke new ground in the areas of the nature and design of government. In fact, West was one of a long line of preacher-politicians who related constitutional government to the truths of Scripture.

A bedrock Puritan political principle stated that God ruled over men by divine constitution. That constitution guaranteed English liberty, so sincerely cherished by the colonists. Government was the application of constitutional principles. Therefore, it followed that an unconstitutional act was not binding, because God did not expect Christians to obey illegal acts.

Politically oriented preachers, speaking in the language of the Bible to a basically religious people, made resistance a sacred calling. In their various ministerial associations, the New England pastors shared and sharpened their political viewpoints. Then they mounted their pulpits to impress upon their people their duty to join the Lord's army and vanquish the foe. Colonists unhappy with high taxes and British foreign policy gratefully received their teaching.

It is not surprising, therefore, that West closed his sermon with an appeal to his "brethren in the ministry" to urge their parishioners not to pray more, not to study the Scriptures more, but to "study civil government."

"It is part of the work and business of a gospel minister to teach his hearers the duty they owe the magistrates. . . . And while we are animating them to oppose tyranny and arbitrary power, let us inculcate upon them the duty of yielding due obedience to lawful authority. . . . By this means we shall be able to guard them against the extremes of slavish submission to tyrants on one hand, and of sedition and licentiousness on the other." According to West, the colonist should resist the British government. But revolutions can get out of hand. The minister of God should place a restraining hand on the revolutionary's shoulder and caution, "Go this far, but no further. Let all things be done in moderation so that your Father in heaven will be glorified."

As Dr. Baldwin points out, the colonial clergy lived, moved and had their being with the people—the "movers and the shakers" as well as with the common folk. The influential Boston clergy socialized and talked revolution with the "faction" promoting revolt. The political leaders may have declared independence, but the ministers turned the revolt into a holy war.

TWELVE

The American Holy War

We may fault the colonial clergymen for their zeal in promoting a violent revolution, but few fall prey to the charge of inconsistency. Many practiced what they preached and either fought shoulder-to-shoulder with the field troops or enlisted as combat chaplains.

Often those who stayed behind also served by preaching patriotic sermons to promote the war effort, boldly challenging the men in their congregations to take up arms and join their brothers in the field. The patriotic clergy put a biblical interpretation on battle victories to reassure the fainthearted that God would never forsake them. With such slogans as, "Resistance to tyrants is obedience to God," they practically guaranteed men facing battle entry into heaven, if they died in defense of God and country.

Some ministers did not endorse the war, but they were the exceptions. In general the clergy locked step with the Whig politicians and gave their blessings to the war effort. The Puritan preachers were far more effective than army recruiters in rounding up citizen-soldiers.

The American army was blessed with fighting parsons

and prayer warriors, who considered prayer as essential to victory in the battlefield as keeping one's powder dry. They pulled no punches in these militaristic prayers. One zealous minister implored the Lord of Hosts to drown the enemy troops at sea before they could reach the mainland. (The American navy was ineffective at this point.) But if the Redcoats *did* make it safely across the Atlantic, then he called upon God to strike them down with bolts of lightning on dry land.

Historian J. T. Headley, the nineteenth-century apologist of the Puritan clergy's role in the American Revolution, admitted that the timid would be appalled by such militant prayers. But Headley believed the colonial ministers merely were being honest by asking God flat out to zap the invaders. He candidly commented: "In these days of peace and security one is apt to look upon such a prayer with profound surprise, if not with condemnation; but the patriotic clergy of the Revolution never practiced self-deception; they did not wish for one thing in their hearts and pray for another with their lips. When they wanted the destruction of their foes, they did not pray about something else, and wait to see if their desires might not be accomplished through the agency of wicked men, or chance or the devil. They came boldly to the very Holy of Holies, and *asked for it*."[1]

After all, the militant minister could point to examples in the Old Testament where God caused the enemies of Israel to throw down their spears and run. More often than not, though, God commanded the Israelites to slaughter the pagan tribes with the sword. The Puritan clergy saw America as the New Israel, and they were willing to place their own lives on the line to back up that belief. Following are accounts of some who marched off to war as Christian soldiers to fight in what they considered to be a holy war.

It had to be one of the strangest send-offs for any American army in military annals. Chaplain Samuel Spring had just finished preaching a fiery, patriotic sermon to troops assembled under the daring leadership of General Benedict Arnold.

The Continental Congress, in secret session, had decided to conquer Quebec and had selected the brilliant field commander to head the troops from Massachusetts, Connecticut, and Rhode Island in the fall of 1775. It was an all-volunteer brigade to carry out a dangerous mission. The 1,100-man force had assembled in Newburyport, Massachusetts, where they would embark on 200 boats for the trip north.

Spring, then thirty years old, had volunteered to accompany the troops.

The young chaplain, fresh out of the College of New Jersey, seems to have been inspired by the fact that the tomb of evangelist George Whitefield was directly beneath the pulpit on which he was standing.

Following his sermon, Chaplain Spring asked General Arnold, a younger officer, Aaron Burr, and several other military aides to go with him to Whitefield's musty tomb.

Then Spring performed a ritual he would never forget—and he was sure later the Lord could never forgive. . . .

As the others watched, not knowing quite what to expect, Chaplain Spring took the lid from Whitefield's coffin. The body had deteriorated. The funeral clothes had returned to dust, except for Whitefield's collar and wrist bands.

Chaplain Spring solemnly removed the collar and wrist bands from the interior of the dusty coffin, cut them in small pieces, and divided them among the startled officers. Then the chaplain prayed to the Lord of battles that "If thy spirit go not with us, carry us not up hence."

The veneration of relics of dead saints was almost unheard of in anti-Catholic New England during the time of the Revolution. This sharing of the talismans, however, was an example—although rather morbid—of the extent to which the patriot clergy went to curry God's favor on their military missions.

If Spring had believed that Whitefield's intercession would guarantee the military success of the mission, he was headed for deep disappointment. When the Americans attempted to attack, a furious snowstorm raged and two feet of snow already blanketed the ground. Arnold, leading his men, was hit in the leg by a musket ball. Chaplain Spring helped the surgeon carry Arnold out of the line of the fire. Arnold turned his command over General Richard Montgomery, who was mortally wounded. Burr carried the dying Montgomery from the field.

The Americans retreated and remained in camp the rest of the winter. In the spring they resumed the offensive, but with no success. Fresh troops arrived from England, smallpox broke out in the American camps, and at length the Americans were driven out of Canada.

The young chaplain, baffled by the turn of events, resigned his army commission and returned to Newburyport. He was appointed minister of the church where he had invoked the blessing of a dead man on the American army.

Spring would serve the church for forty-two years and never forget the unusual ritual he had performed before Benedict Arnold led his troops out to defeat. Yet he always had the uneasy feeling that the "Lord of Battles had been outraged by such blasphemous, un-Protestant conduct" and that probably accounted for the failure of the mission.

Timothy Dwight was a child prodigy, who read the Bible with ease at four and began studying Latin at six. He entered Yale at thirteen but spent most of his first two years in college gambling—though not for money—and in other nonspiritual pleasures. A concerned tutor persuaded Timothy to give up gambling and take life more seriously, upon which the straying student made a 180-degree turn and began studying fourteen hours a day. In fact, he studied so long and intensely that he began to have eye trouble. He graduated from Yale at seventeen and enlisted as a chaplain with the American army at the age of twenty-five in 1777—the same year Yale disbanded because of the threat from British troops.

In the vanguard of lovers of liberty, Timothy Dwight took proper pride in the fact that he urged the colonies to break from England at least a whole year before the Declaration of Independence was issued. "For myself," he recalled later, "I regarded the die as cast, and the hope of reconciliation as vanished, and believed that the Colonists would never be able to defend themselves unless they renounced their dependence on Great Britain."

Dwight "threw himself heart and soul into the contest." He was named chaplain to serve with General Israel Putnam, an aging veteran of the old French and Indian War. At a time when things were going badly for the colonists, "Gentleman Johnny" Burgoyne was defeated near Saratoga by Major General Horatio Gates's forces. When news of the defeat of the British northern army reached "Old Put's" camp, the Americans were elated. In those dark hours they desperately needed a victory.

The day after the news of victory had been delivered, Dwight preached at Putnam's headquarters. General Putnam and his entire staff were present. Dwight, sure Gates's victory came from the hand of the Lord, took for his text Joel 2:20, 21: *"I will remove far off from you the northern army.* . . . Fear not, O land; be glad and rejoice: for the Lord will do great things" (italics added).

To the patriotic preacher, Joel's prophecy spoke directly to Burgoyne's defeat. Describing the American victory, Dwight gave God all the glory, while assuring his attentive listeners that Saratoga was a sure sign of final triumph.

"Old Put" smiled and nodded all through the sermon. He was impressed with Dwight's youthful enthusiasm—but he was convinced his young chaplain had manufactured his own text.

After the service, General Putnam loudly praised the sermon and the preacher. Emphasizing that he knew there was no such text in the Bible, the crusty general said it was still a good show for all that. When his staff argued that Dwight really *had* been quoting Scripture, Putnam asked that they show him chapter and verse—which they did. Taking the Bible into his own hands and reading the text himself, Putnam recovered by announcing: "Well, there is everything in that book, and Dwight knows just where to lay his finger on it."

Timothy Dwight was a poet as well as a preacher. While still caught up in the rapture of the success at Saratoga, he composed an ode that begins:

> *Columbia! Columbia! to glory arise,*
> *Thou queen of the world, and child of the skies.*

Dwight reflected the feeling of his copatriots in the second verse, which rather self-righteously asserts:

> *To conquest and slaughter let Europe aspire,*
> *Whelm nations in blood, and wrap cities in fire;*
> *Thy heroes the rights of mankind shall defend,*
> *and triumph pursue them, and glory attend.*

Dwight left the army in 1779 and, like so many ministers, became active in politics. He represented Northampton in 1781–1782 in the general court of Massachusetts, and in 1795 he was elected President of Yale College.

One of the most powerful "preachers" in the American Revolution was the Reverend Judah Champion, pastor of the Congregationalist parish of Litchfield, Connecticut. His prayers caused the spines of patriots to tingle. By the time the American Revolution came along, Pastor Champion was no novice at communicating with God. During his studies at Yale, he had only missed prayers once—and that because he had been given extra duty by a spiritually obtuse senior. His ability as a fervent pray-er was a legend among his parishioners. When anyone became ill, they always called for their pastor to accompany the physician and apply his spiritual ministrations along with the doctor's medicine.

During the war, a regiment of cavalry once attended Champion's Sunday service. As he looked out into the pews at those young men who faced death daily to preserve the faith on American shores, his piety and patriotism blended to produce an unsurpassed appeal to the Lord of battle.

Champion reminded the Lord that if the British successfully conquered the colonies, religion as revealed in the Bible would lie in ruins. Congregations would be scattered, churches burned, and the Lord's own people would become a "hissing and a by-word among their foes."

Then Champion became more precise: "O Lord, we view with terror and dismay the enemies of our holy religion; wilt thou send storm and tempest to toss them upon the seas, to overwhelm them in the mighty deep, or scatter them to the utmost parts of the earth. But, peradventure, should they escape thy vengeance, collect them together again, O Lord, as in the hollow of thy hand, and let thy lightnings play upon them."

Champion then asked God to provide the same protection for the American army as He had done in the past for the Israelites. After all, many of the clergy saw America as the Promised Land and Americans as the Chosen People.

Champion recognized that many Americans—perhaps one of those very men sitting out in front of him—would be killed in action. He asked that those who would be killed in combat be ushered through gates of splendor prepared for those who give their lives in a holy war.

"If on the other hand, thou hast decreed they shall die in battle, let thy spirit be present with them that they may go up as a sweet sacrifice into the courts of thy temple, where are habitations prepared for them from the foundation of the world."

One cold morning in late November, 1775, when the village of Litchfield gathered for worship, a man on horseback rode up at breakneck speed. The messenger walked down the center aisle of the meetinghouse, in the midst of the service, with the gravity of one bearing an important message. He handed the Reverend Champion a note. The pastor quickly scanned it and with joyful voice shared the message with his congregation. "St. John's is taken! Thank God for the victory!" The chorister, unable to contain his own emotions, clapped his hands and shouted, "Amen, and Amen!" St.

John's had been under American siege for eight weeks and was seen as the gateway to the conquest of Canada.

But there was more to the message. It told how the American army suffered lack of clothing. Many men walked the frozen earth with their feet wrapped only in rags. The women in the congregation wiped the tears from their eyes as they heard of the shocking condition of the American troops. But they did more than weep. After the service ended, they gathered in excited groups and covenanted to spend Sunday afternoon spinning, knitting, and sewing clothing for the men at the front.

The Puritan Sabbath usually included two sermons a day—morning and afternoon—with working strictly prohibited. But the women obviously had the blessing of their pastor. So while he preached to an all-male assembly in the afternoon, the women stayed home and tended to their knitting. The hum of the spinning wheel along with the clash of the shuttle made "strange harmony with the worship of the sanctuary."

Judah Champion's blessing on the breaking of the Sabbath became a minor family scandal. Many years later, when he was questioned about it by a granddaughter, the doughty old prayer warrior replied: "Mercy before sacrifice."

"The Bible tells us 'there is a time for all things' and there is a time to preach and a time to pray but the time for me to preach has passed away." These words of the Reverend John Peter Gabriel Muhlenberg, a Lutheran pastor in Virginia's Shenandoah Valley, startled his congregation one Sunday morning in 1776.

The fiery minister, soon to become one of the best-known "fighting parsons," then raised his voice to a near shout, thundering: "There is a time to fight, and that time has now come!"

His parishioners knew he was a superpatriot, but they were not prepared for what happened next. Muhlenberg stepped out of the pulpit into the adjoining vestry room and removed his clerical garb to reveal a Virginia colonel's uniform. He then walked down the aisle to the front door.

"Roll the drums for recruits!" he ordered.

The drummer boy broke the Sabbath silence with his tattoo, and the congregation stood. No able-bodied man dared hesitate or lag behind. The men walked out the front door to enlist in their former pastor's Eighth Virginia Regiment.

As the drum beat continued, all those within hearing distance rushed to the church to see what was going on. "The sight of the pastor in uniform," J. T. Headley wrote, "standing at the door and calling for recruits, kindled the most unbounded enthusiasm, and before night nearly 300 men had joined his standard." Muhlenberg immediately moved his regiment south to join in the battle of Charleston.

Muhlenberg easily switched from the ministry to the military. He rose rapidly in the ranks. The next year he was promoted to the rank of brigadier general and placed in command of all the Continental troops in Virginia. He later was attached to General Washington's staff. He led his troops through some of the war's fiercest battles—Brandywine, Germantown, and Yorktown.

His own brother, Frederick, also a clergyman, criticized him for taking up arms. "You say as a clergyman nothing can excuse my conduct," Muhlenberg rebutted. "I am a clergyman, it is true, but I am a member of society as well as the poorest layman, and my liberty is as dear to me as any man.

Shall I then sit still, and enjoy myself at home, when the best blood of the continent is spilling? Heaven forbid it!"

If heaven did forbid it, Muhlenberg never got the message. As he told his brother, "I am convinced it is my duty so to do, a duty I owe to God and my country."

It was a point of view few would challenge.

One could easily argue that the patriotic clergy of the American Revolution were too quick to shoot from the lip. They injected large doses of Whig ideas and doctrine into their politically flavored sermons. They were responsible for many Americans marching off to war. They flew in tight formation with the war hawks. However, many paid with their lives for what they believed. Presbyterian pastor James Caldwell gave his life, his wife, and his property for the American cause.

A short, muscular man, Caldwell had a voice that could be "low, sweet and musical, captivating the hearers by its winning tone." His voice also could take on the snarl of a drill sergeant, sounding loud and clear "over the roll of the drums and the piercing notes of the fife."

Caldwell's historic moment came in New Jersey, when the colonials were running out of wadding to ram their muskets. In the thick of the fray, Caldwell, "seeing the fire of one of the companies slackening for want of wadding, he galloped to the Presbyterian meetinghouse nearby, and rushing in, ran from pew to pew, filling his arms with hymnbooks." Arms full, he ran outside and remounted.

The preacher then charged back into the battle, scattering hymn books and shouting, "Now put 'Watts' into them, boys, put 'Watts' into them.'' (Isaac Watts composed many of the church hymns.)

Caldwell's Presbyterian church in Elizabethtown, New Jersey, was a hothouse of rebellion. The state's leading rebels were members of his congregation. One of his parishioners was named commander of the New Jersey brigade, and Caldwell was elected chaplain. When the news trickled down on July 15 that the nation's leaders had issued a Declaration of Independence, the soldiers celebrated the news with a "barrel of grog,'' with Chaplain Caldwell giving the toast.

Caldwell fought the war on all fronts—from the pulpit on the Lord's Day, in the army during the week, and debating with Tories and encouraging the weakhearted in his spare time.

His vocal support won him the undying enmity of the British, who offered large rewards for his capture. When the British took New York and Staten Island, he moved his family to a farm in Connecticut.

Caldwell always carried side arms and boasted that no four men could take him alive. Often before starting a worship service, he would unbuckle a brace of pistols, place them in front of him, and begin to preach. "He was engaged in what he firmly believed to be the cause of God,'' Headley wrote. "And that cause he did not consider would be advanced by yielding himself unresistingly into the hands of a skulking Tory to be dragged to the scaffold.''

Once while Caldwell was off to war, the British began sacking the town where his wife and small children lived. A British Redcoat jumped over the fence and shot through the window, killing Mrs. Caldwell. The soldiers then set the parsonage on fire. Neighbors dragged Mrs. Caldwell's body out of the burning building but had to flee for their own safety.

While in camp, Caldwell learned of the tragedy. Concerned about his children, he secured a flag of truce and rode back to his Connecticut farm. The village was a smoking ruin, but he found the body of his wife. His terrified children, one of whom was a baby, had been given shelter in a nearby house.

Caldwell buried his wife, placed his children in the care of a neighbor, and rushed back to join the army at Springfield, New Jersey. During the battle that followed Caldwell uttered his famous cry, "Put 'Watts' into them, boys."

Caldwell met his death at the hands of an American sentry, a member of his own New Jersey militia. The man who shot him was James Morgan, the local drunk, who received a drumhead court-martial. Evidence was introduced showing that Morgan was actually not on duty at the time but had already been relieved. Some say Morgan felt angry because he had not been paid and blamed Caldwell, who was the militia commissary as well as chaplain. Others say the British bribed him. Anyway he was hanged.

Congress's tradition of beginning its proceedings with prayer almost died aborning. The patriots of the Continental Congress, who met in Philadelphia on September 5, 1774, to talk revolution were a religious mix—Congregationalists, Presbyterians, Anglicans, Quakers, and Baptists.

Wily Sam Adams, wanted to avoid any impression that the radicals from Boston dominated the Congress. So as a sop to the southerners—all of whom were members of the Church of England—he suggested that an Anglican rector be asked to invoke God's blessing on the Congress and the cause of freedom.

Adams's motion was met with mixed reaction. Several delegates objected that because of the differing denominations represented, they all "could not join in the same act of worship."

But Sam Adams proved that even a politician can rise above his principles when it serves his purpose. His cousin, John Adams, an inveterate letter writer, described the historic scene in a letter to his wife, Abigail:

> Mr. Sam Adams arose, and said, "He was no bigot, and could hear a prayer from a gentleman of piety and virtue, who was at the same time a friend to his country. He (Adams) was a stranger in Philadelphia, but had heard that Mr. Duche (Dushay they pronounce it) deserved that character, and he therefore moved that Mr. Duche, an Episcopal clergyman, might be desired to read prayers to the Congress tomorrow morning." The motion was seconded and passed in the affirmative.

Sam Adams left the session pleased with his prayer motion. But if the patriot had been as good a prophet as he was a politician, he would have known he had made a major mistake.

The Reverend Jacob Duché accepted the request of Congress to pray over it and appeared the next morning in clerical garb. His performance was superb.

The members of Congress were in a state of agitation. They had heard—and believed—the false rumor that the British had turned their cannons on Boston. Duché, aware of the apprehension and tension of the hour, tailored his words to fit the occasion. After reading the thirty-fifth Psalm, he launched into a spontaneous prayer—highly unusual for an Anglican. Again, John Adams sent an on-the-scene report to Abigail:

I must confess I never heard a better prayer or one so well pronounced. Episcopalian as he [Duché] is, Dr. Cooper [Adams was so excited he misplaced his modifier: Cooper was his Congregational pastor back in Boston] never prayed with such ardor, such earnestness and pathos, and in language so eloquent and sublime for America, for Congress, for the province of Massachusetts Bay, and especially the town of Boston. It has had an excellent effect upon everybody here.

"Defeat the malicious designs of our cruel adversaries," Duché requested of God. "Convince them of the unrighteousness of their cause." If the British could not be convinced of their wrongheaded course, then Duché asked God to escalate His intervention in behalf of the colonies by letting "the voice of thine own unerring justice sounding in their hearts constrain them to drop the weapons of war from their unnerved hands in the day of battle."

Throughout 1775 and 1776, Duché continued to hold the torch of liberty high. About two weeks after the battle of Bunker Hill, the Anglican rector addressed the troops of the First Battalion of Philadelphia in Christ Church. He used the text that had become standard among ministers who were whipping up the spirit of resistance: "Stand fast therefore, in the liberty wherewith Christ hath made us free."

Duché's patriotism did not go unnoticed. A few days after the signing of the Declaration of Independence, he was informed that "the Congress of the United States had appointed him their chaplain and would be pleased to have him attend on them every morning at nine o'clock."

For the next three months the Anglican rector showed up promptly at 9:00 A.M. to beseech the Almighty to join hands with the thirteen colonies and wipe out the British invaders. "To these have they appealed for their righteousness of their cause," he prayed, "to these do they now look up for that countenance and support which thou alone can give."

But even as Duché's patriotic prayers ascended heavenward, the British won victories on the battlefield. It was the kind of time that tried men's souls, and Duché's soul was sorely pressed. The closer the British advanced toward Philadelphia, the cooler Duché's ardor for his country became. When the king's troops occupied Philadelphia, Duché "promptly turned the political coat which he wore under his surplice."

Not content to switch his allegiance and silently steal away, Duché compounded his treachery by writing a letter to General Washington, asking him to resign his command of the army. If Washington didn't want to resign, Duché urged him to pull off a military coup and force Congress to rescind its Declaration of Independence and contritely return to the British fold.

"If this is not done," the patriot-turned-traitor stated, "you have an infallible resource still left—negotiate for America at the head of your Army."

The former chaplain of the Continental Congress then berated the very body he had prayed over so fervently. He was especially contemptuous of the New England delegates, and he asserted that American army officers were destitute of principle and courage and were not worthy to sit at the same table as Washington.

Outraged by the suggestions made by the former chaplain of Congress, Washington told the bearer of Duché's letter that had he known what the contents were, he would not have opened it. Having opened it, Washington said he felt it his duty to turn it over to Congress so they could take the proper action against the man they had honored as their first chaplain.

As the tide turned in the Revolutionary War and Americans

began winning some battles, Duché found it unsafe to remain in Philadelphia and fled to England, to become a chaplain in an orphanage. He never returned to the City of Brotherly Love until tempers had cooled in 1790—seven years after the shooting had stopped. He died four years later.

Other ministers unswervingly spoke out against the break with Great Britain from the beginning and never wavered in their convictions. Some left the land they loved rather than compromise their principles. They were, and still are, considered traitors. But they saw themselves as loyal citizens trying to stem a tide of lawlessness. They believed armed revolt violated Scripture as well as the English Constitution. They were out of step with the times and paid a terrible price. Their lives were threatened and their property appropriated by the rebels. They were dragged before misnamed Councils of Safety and ordered to recant their political beliefs or flee the country. It was the dark side of the American Revolution—the missing chapter in our history books. It, too, needs to be told.

THIRTEEN

The Other Side

"**W**ho shall write the history of the American Revolution? Who will be able to write it?" John Adams questioned Thomas Jefferson, writing thirty-nine years after the signing of the Declaration of Independence. Adams surely knew that winners of wars always write the history books.

Americans have been so indoctrinated by the Whig view of the American Revolution that we forget our textbooks have been shaped by a partisan point of view. There really are *two* sides to the American Revolution. But how many schoolchildren peek at the loyalist side of the conflict? How many history books have you read on the American Revolution written by a British historian or an American loyalist?

As the editors of *Peter Oliver's Origin and Progress of the American Rebellion* point out in their introduction:

> One difficulty in writing a balanced history of the American Revolution arises in part from its success as a creator of our nation and our nationalistic sentiment. The revolution is a historic event that all Americans applaud today as both necessary and desirable.
>
> One of the results, however, of this happy unanimity on the

desirable consequences of the civil war and revolution that began in 1775 is that the chief loser—the American Loyalists—have fared badly at the hands of historians. It was nearly a hundred years after the revolution before the extremely heterdox opinion was advanced by Lorenzo Sabine that the Loyalists were not all devils. It has only been in the last fifty years that a scattering of monographs and biographies have attempted to do justice to their position.[1]

Historians present their cases much in the same manner as a lawyer makes his closing argument in a jury trial. But in order to deal logically with a subject a historian focuses on a specific thesis and sifts and selects evidence to support it. We don't call this biased or lopsided, however; we say the historian belongs to a certain school of thought that holds a particular view. The Whig school has dominated our history books.

Attempting an overview of the role of religion in the American Revolution without calling any loyalists to the stand would be unfair. After all, John Adams estimated that one-third of the colonists remained loyal to the crown during the War of Independence. Thousands were forced to flee their homeland to escape the fury of the patriot mobs who stole their possessions and appropriated their estates.

Because loyalists often were in the upper income brackets of colonial society, their secure status made it difficult for them to accurately gauge the depth of the rebellion spreading across the land. Slow to believe what their ears heard and their eyes saw, suddenly they found themselves caught up in a firestorm of resistance that they never understood and that they regarded as pure madness.

As they sought refuge aboard British frigates the bewildered loyalists consoled themselves with the vain beliefs that the world's strongest army soon would put down the rebellion and they would return to America to live out their lives under the protection of the king.

The other side of this study will include firsthand testimony of two prominent Tories—one a politician and the other an Anglican rector. Both held responsible positions in colonial society before the outbreak of hostilities. One was a personal friend of George Washington and the other a close friend of John Adams. Both blamed the Puritan clergy for whipping up the populace and preaching politics; both eventually left America for the security of England; and both, because they chose the wrong side, ended up as historical footnotes.

Our witnesses are Peter Oliver, the veteran jurist who became Chief Justice of the Superior Court of Massachusetts, and Jonathan Boucher, an abrasive, arrogant, but fearless Church of England rector.

Too often loyalists have been simplistically tagged *traitors* by Whig historians. The loyalist, of course, saw himself in a different light. He believed the real traitors were those attempting to overthrow a legally constituted government, which, while not perfect, was still the best ever devised by flawed and imperfect men.

Even if one believes the loyalists were misguided, it does not necessarily follow that they also were malicious and spiteful creatures eager to bend the knee to a petty monarch rather than fight for the right in a glorious revolution. Hundreds of loyalists left the country, stunned and uncomprehending that a people could be so ungrateful to a government that so generously and fairly administered the colonies.

England had spilled its blood and spent millions protecting the colonies from the attacks of the Indians and the encroachment of the French. Now that the borders had been secured, was it right to turn on one's previous protector? Many

Americans did not think so and risked life, limb, and property to remain loyal. They knew they were among the freest men on the globe. Surely reasonable men could sit down and come to a reasonable solution over even genuine grievances without taking up arms and resisting.

Let's give the loyalists a fair hearing. We shall now call to the stand our first witness for the other side.

Peter Oliver was a jurist accustomed to adversarial trial proceedings. A judge in the Massachusetts courts for years, Oliver capped his legal career by being named chief justice of the superior court of that state. He served as one of the judges in the trial of the British Redcoats charged in the riot we now call the Boston Massacre. John Adams, to his credit, served as a defense attorney for the British soldiers.

A man of extensive holdings, including an iron foundry, Oliver moved in the inner circle of the Massachusetts power structure. He was an intimate advisor to Governor Thomas Hutchinson and served in the same capacity to General Thomas Gage, commander in chief of the British forces in America, when Gage was appointed military governor of Massachusetts in 1774. No one ever doubted where Oliver's sympathies lay, and he never attempted to conceal his allegiance to the crown.

Oliver wrote an eyewitness account of the Revolution while in exile in England in a book he called *Origin and Progress of the American Rebellion*. His manuscript was written in 1781 but was not published here until 1961. In an almost ecstatic footnote in his work *Mitre and Sceptre* historian Carl Bridenbaugh makes this important point:

In a communication of October, 1961, Mr. Adair [Douglass Adair and John A. Schutz edited Oliver's book] drew my attention to the startling parallels between Judge Oliver's account of the Revolution in Massachusetts and that of John Adams as set forth in his celebrated letters to Jedidiah Morse, William Tudor and Benjamin Rush. Both writers date its beginning from 1761, both introducing the same cast of characters, both chose the same catalogue of events, which they view as crucial features of the growing crisis, and both look upon the arousing of "Mr. Otis's black Regiment, the dissenting clergy," as the key to the great agitator's conquest of public opinion.[2]

Oliver's first-person narrative of the causes of the American Revolution is by its very nature passionate, prejudiced, and partisan. He could not find it in his heart to forgive those political firebrands we call our founders, who caused the country to go into convulsions and then like some huge, tormented fish trying to expel a Jonah from its inward parts, spewed from its shores its brightest and best citizens.

The editors of Oliver's account believe, however, that the jurist was an accurate reporter:

> Apparently Oliver based many of his statements, like incidents of tar and feathering, upon newspaper accounts, taken usually from the *Boston Weekly News-Letter*. The quotations that have been located are accurate, and the essential facts in his descriptions are handled with care. Most dates and allusions to events, when they can be checked, are accurate. One is impressed again and again by the care with which Oliver wrote his history.[3]

The editors further emphasized that Oliver had one distinct advantage over latter-day historians, who must view the

American Revolution through a two-hundred-year time prism. Oliver was there when it happened and knew most of the leaders of the patriot party personally. "Unlike present historians, he observed them without the *filter of time* and the advantage of historical evidence that is not available to scholars today."

Oliver is precise in dating the origin of the American rebellion. The year was 1761. King George III had been on the British throne only a year. Thomas Hutchinson had been appointed chief justice of the Province of Massachusetts Bay. James Otis, Sr., his political nemesis, believed he should have been given the post. When he was passed over, Otis was furious, turning his fiery wrath on Hutchinson. When Otis died, his son, James Otis, Jr., took up the vendetta.

"Mr. Otis, the son," wrote Oliver, "advanced one shrewd position, which seldom failed to promote popular commotion, Viz., that it was necessary to seduce the black Regiment; these were his words and his meaning was to engage the dissenting Clergy on his side . . . & this order of men might, in a literal sense, be styled such, for like their predecessors of 1641 [the Cromwell era] they had unceasingly been sounding the yell of Rebellion in the ears of an ignorant and deluded people."

Agreeing with many of his contemporaries, Oliver credits the brilliant but unstable Otis with being the "first who broke down the barrier of government to let in the Hydra of Rebellion." In his later years John Adams would use more flattering terms as he recalled how Otis spoke for four hours in a "torrent of eloquence" against the British writs of assistance. Mesmerized by Otis's courtroom performance, Adams, then a young lawyer, wrote: "Then and there, the child Independence was born." One man's baby was another man's hydra, in 1776.

Even a dyed-in-the-wig Tory like Oliver would have subscribed to John Locke's theory of revolution: The oppressed have a natural right to overthrow their oppressors and start all over again by setting up a government of their own design and choice. But to Oliver it was unthinkable that the British oppressed his fellow citizens. He could concede there were grievances. However, men of reason and goodwill could settle those kind of disagreements without overthrowing the government.

Oliver regarded the growing refusal of the stubborn colonists to accept British authority as treasonous. By then the colonists' feeling that they had no one but themselves to answer to had spread like burning lava across the land, undermining British institutions and igniting revolutions everywhere. As Oliver looked around him, he clearly saw why the colonies were headed for revolt: Men of flawed character held positions of leadership. Ministers preached Whig politics instead of the gospel of peace and nonresistance. Respect for one's natural superiors had vanished. A "leveling" spirit had infected every plowboy, who saw himself either as a patriot without peer or as a preacher called by God to chastise the morally bankrupt British. Every man did what was right in his own eyes—which always leads to moral decay and lawlessness, Oliver argued.

An ardent advocate of law and order, Oliver blamed the British policy of appeasement for the loss of the American colonies. He was convinced that had the king and Parliament clamped down on the colonies at the outset, the unruly element would have been subdued, and the majority of citizens would have been happy to bask under the never-setting British sun. He bitterly criticized Edmund Burke and William Pitt, who often defended the Americans on the floor of the British Parliament.

Oliver paints Sam Adams in the blackest colors in his rogue's gallery of misguided militants. He faulted Adams for his close association with the lower social class, charging him with pocketing public monies when he was the town clerk of Boston, and accused old Sam of being a religious hypocrite who more closely resembled Satan than he did an angel of light.

Oliver depicts John Hancock as a lightweight whose head was filled with importance while his mentor Adams picked his pockets. Hancock's mind was a "meer Tabula Rasa [clean slate]" soon filled with the revolutionary graffiti of Sam Adams.

The Congregational clergy, in Oliver's view, formed the core of the leadership of the Revolution. Oliver viewed the clergy "in general, a set of very weak men . . . tinctured with Republicanism."

Boston was the seat of sedition, and in this metropolis the clergy held sway. "And hence it was that their clergy being dependent on the people for their daily bread, by having frequent intercourse with the people, imbibed their principles."[4] It was only a short step from Republicanism to revolution in Oliver's tunnel vision.

The big three in Boston's radical clerical circle were Dr. Charles Chauncy, Dr. Jonathan Mayhew, and Dr. Samuel Cooper. "And they distinguished themselves," Oliver wrote, "in encouraging seditions and riots, until those lesser offences were absorbed in rebellion."

Charles Chauncy (1705–1787) was the most influential of the "sacerdotal Triumvirate." He was the son of a Boston merchant and served the prestigious First Church for sixty years. Chauncy was seventy-one years old when the Americans declared their independence, but age did not diminish his patriotic zeal. The outspoken preacher freely admitted he was able to curb his passionate outbursts in his sermons only by writing them down and always keeping a blotter handy.

"His hoary head had great respect paid to it by the factions and seditions," laments Oliver. "And it would have really been a crown of glory to him had it been found in the way of righteousness." Oliver's vignette of Chauncy (which never actually mentions his name) reveals the influence of the venerable minister as it illuminates Oliver's contempt for men of the cloth who pandered to the patriots: "One clergyman in Boston, in particular who seemed to be devoted to an abstraction from the world, and had gone through an existence of nearly 70 years, reputedly free from both original sin and actual transgression, yet by perpetual buzzing of incendiaries at his ear, being inquired of as an oracle, 'what ought to be done by the people?' He uttered his decision with the laconick [sic] answer, 'Fight up to your knees in blood.' "

Jonathan Mayhew is credited by Oliver (one feels rather grudgingly) as being a man of "strong reason" but still flawed by "too great a share of pride for an humble disciple of so divine a master, and looked with too contemptuous an eye on all around him."

Samuel Cooper, of the Brattle Square Church, earned the enmity of the Tories by speaking out against the Stamp Act. Oliver saw Cooper as a superficial person not deep in his profession (the ministry) but very deep in the black art (fomenting rebellion). He was the close correspondent of men like Samuel Adams, Dr. Joseph Warren, and Benjamin Franklin.

"No man could," Oliver wrote, "with a better grace utter the word of God from his mouth, and at the same time keep a two-edged dagger concealed in his hand." The young Dr. Cooper's pleasant facade only angered Oliver. "His manners were such that he was always agreeable to the politest company, who were unacquainted with his real character,

[but] he could descend from them to mix privately with the rabble, in their nightly seditious associations."

Having completed his word portraits of the unholy trio of perverse patriots, Oliver indulged his sarcastic humor by suggesting to his readers: "If you like them and think them ornamental for your parlor, pray hang them in it; for I assure you, that most of them justly demerit a suspension."

The British Parliament's repeal of the Stamp Act, which had threatened to plunge the colonies into revolt, convinced the revolutionary leaders that they could indeed change the course of human events. As the most visible representative of the British government in the colonies, the governor made the best target. The patriots branded him as the archenemy and treated him as a royal hireling, defaming his reputation and plundering his household.

Citizens thumbed their noses at British rule by buying smuggled goods from merchants who refused to import British goods. "The inhabitants of the colonies were a race of smugglers," Oliver observed scornfully.

Any form of British authority was continually challenged and frustrated. Local assemblies and state bodies were packed with patriots, who purged loyalists from their ranks. Mobs intimidated juries and judges who tried to maintain a semblance of law and order. Newspapers openly labeled officials, using epithets like "limping dog" or "Tom Cod."

Governor Hutchinson tried to maintain a form of government long after mob rule had in reality replaced it. Boston now was an occupied city, and tension between the citizens and soldiers seemed stuck near the flash point.

Respect for British rule went overboard with the tea in the Boston Tea Party. Now two irreconcilable factions were pitted against each other, and the American Revolution was ready to begin. Home rule had replaced British rule; local residents formed associations and committees that carried more clout among the ordinary citizens than did the British authorities. For the British, events had reached the point Oliver described in the idiom of the day as "Neck or Nothing." There was no turning back. England's role in the New World was giving away to a new order, which would be ushered in by violence and bloodshed.

As those events transpired before his unbelieving eyes, Oliver saw the heavy hand of the clergy stoking the fire of revolution. He could never forgive either James Otis, Jr., or the Puritan clergy who preached unnatural rebellion against Mother England: "Mr. Otis's black regiment, the dissenting Clergy, were also sent to work, to preach up manufacturing [of American goods] instead of the Gospel.

"The clergy supported the rabble—one minister seeing the rabble breaking the windows of one who had imported English goods, exclaimed, 'See how those boys fight for us.'

"The garrets now were crowded with the rabble in full divan, with a clergyman to preside, whose part was to declaim on politics and sedition, instead of propagating the gospel of peace. Had the force of enthusiasm been well understood & what power the dissenting clergy had over the minds of the people in America, it would have been a great error in politicks [sic] not to have suppressed the growth of such a weed [rebellion] as hath poisoned both Old and New England."

Oliver had sound financial reasons for his enthusiasm for the British rule in the colonies. A member of one of the best families in New England, with powerful connections and vast holdings, "he owned extensive property at Middleborough that rivaled any in New England, with a great house on a hill, a library occupying one wing, gardens, orchards, and grain fields spreading from it, and an iron foundry that made him master of an eighteenth-century industrial complex."[5]

Oliver had prospered under the system and obviously wanted it to continue. But when General Gage sealed off Boston, he joined the other loyalists who fled to Boston for safety. Soon Oliver found himself on the inside looking out. His world had been turned upside down. He ended his days in suburban London, living in a small cottage, with several other New England exiles as neighbors, wondering what happened.

"His few surviving letters show little bitterness, except that he was bewildered as most exiles were by the success of the revolution, and by its complete overturn of their career and life expectations, and he wondered at its cause. He could see God's punishment in the later madness of Otis and Hawley, the ruined estates of Hancock, and the early death of Warren and others. But he could not help asking himself how the revolution occurred and why he was an exile."[6]

In that question and in exile, he would be joined by another loyalist, dragged under by the current of events he could neither understand nor control.

Now we call our second witness for the other side.

As he made his way toward the pulpit on that fast day of 1775, the Reverend Jonathan Boucher carried a loaded pistol and a sermon carefully written to avoid offending the fire-breathing patriots in his St. Anne's Parish, Maryland.

An Anglican rector and an undaunted loyalist in Whig-controlled Prince George's County, Maryland, Boucher knew he was in trouble when he arrived at the church fifteen minutes before the service. More than two hundred armed men had taken over the church, encouraged by the preaching of his own young assistant, a Whig firebrand, and led by his personal enemy, Colonel Osborne Sprigg.

But Boucher was not easily intimidated. He believed in meeting danger head-on. The target of threats and harassment by local committees of patriots, he had responded by preaching with a pair of loaded pistols at his side, publicly serving notice that anyone who dared to drag him from the pulpit would have to face the consequences.

We rarely read how oppressive the Whig zealots of the eighteenth century really were. In many ways the fear that prevailed among suspected Tories sounds unlike what we usually think of as the spirit of '76.

"As the revolutionary movement gained momentum, extra legal committees became the nerve system of the entire operation," Anne Y. Zimmer wrote in her revealing book, *Jonathan Boucher: Loyalist in Exile*. She describes the attitude of the Whig party spirit in words that grate on modern ears:

> Meanwhile, the local committees were arrogating to themselves the functions of the local government, and in their enthusiasm often resorting to vigilantism or outright terrorism. They served as the eyes and ears of the Continental Association, ferreting out violators, publishing their names and misdeeds to the community, and persuading them by various means to mend their ways. By 1776 scarcely any aspect of daily life remained beyond committee scrutiny. As part of the effort to detect and silence political sentiment "inimical to the cause of America," the committees of observation, as the local committees became known, intercepted mail and censored it, monitored opinions expressed both privately and publicly, and scrutinized questionable associates."[7]

The Maryland Convention had even passed a resolution to the effect that those who refused to contribute funds for arms and ammunition or refused to enroll in a military unit had to either leave their homes or be disarmed and post a bond as a guarantee against treason.

Boucher, called before a committee in Annapolis, had agreed to turn in his arms—but obviously not all of them. He still kept a brace of pistols for personal protection. He had one of them on him when he entered his church on that fast day.

Sizing up the armed men who had invaded the sanctuary, Boucher knew his moment of truth had come. He prepared to mount the pulpit "with my sermon in one hand and a loaded pistol in the other."[8] A friend threw his arms around him, warning in a low voice that twenty marksmen had been ordered to fire at the stubborn minister if he had the audacity to ascend into the pulpit. But Boucher insisted he had the right to his own pulpit. Several in the church agreed with him; others, fearing bloodshed, tried to block his path. The sanctuary became the scene of shouted threats and violent jostling. The gun-toting patriots under Sprigg quickly shoved the moderates aside and surrounded the minister.

Seizing the initiative, Boucher grabbed Sprigg by the collar "and with my cocked pistol in the other hand, assured him that if any violence were offered to me, I would instantly blow his brains out.

"I then told him he might conduct me to my horse and I would leave them." The parade to Boucher's horse, one hundred yards away, developed into a musical comedy. In front was Boucher, walking behind Sprigg, holding a gun to his head. Behind came the militia, two hundred strong and helpless to rescue their hostage-leader. But Sprigg did manage to save some face by ordering his men to play the "Rogue's March" on their drums as the fearless clergyman and his uncomfortable captive made their way toward the tethered horse—the only creature that seemed not to have lost its senses.

Between the years 1763 and 1775—at which time he was forced to flee the country, to England—Boucher opposed the fermenting rebellion with sundry sermons. In 1797, Boucher published a series of his sermons, printed in England under the title *A View of the Causes and Consequences of the American Revolution in Thirteen Discourses Preached in North America Between the Years 1763 and 1775.*

Zimmer pens a warning about Boucher's post-Revolution publication:

> It is hazardous, however, to consider this [Boucher's] book as an accurate representation of Boucher's thought in America because of a problem in dating the sermons. In spite of Boucher's assurances that his opinions had undergone no change, his contemporary correspondence indicates otherwise. . . . It is clear that some of the published sermons purporting to have been delivered in America were reconstructions which Boucher developed from minimal notes."[9]

The point is well taken. But the discourses and an eighty-nine-page preface, which Zimmer states sets "forth one of the first historiographies of the American Revolution," are of immense value in that they give a clear presentation of the other side.

Interestingly, Boucher dedicated his book to George Washington. "I was once," Boucher wrote Washington, "your neighbour and friend; the unhappy dispute, which terminated in the disunion of our respective countries, also broke off our personal connexion: but I never was more than your political enemy and every sentiment even of political animosity has, on my part, long ago subsided."

Then the clergyman added this poignant note: "Permit me then to hope, that this tender of renewed amity between us may be received and regarded as giving some promise of that perfect reconciliation between our two countries which it is the sincere aim of this publication to promote."

Boucher had become rather well acquainted with Colonel Washington by 1768, and they often visited in each other's homes. In 1770, Boucher moved to Annapolis, which he described as "the genteelist town in North America." It was the kind of cultured, class-conscious society Boucher thrived in. The rich came long distances to watch and bet on the thoroughbreds racing at the mile-long track outside the city. Washington stayed with Boucher for the fall festivities in 1771, attending the races and parties in the homes of the Maryland social set.

But Boucher and Washington, both men of wealth, with the same tastes for the good life, held opposing views on the most important issue of the day—the colonies' relationship with Britain. The contention was so sharp that their seven-year friendship gradually evolved into political enmity. By 1775, men had to make choices. Events would not permit them to remain neutral. The only alternative, as Boucher said in his preface, was "to be loyal and be ruined, or to rebel and be damned." He chose to be a loyalist unto the end. His conservative principles would not permit him to do otherwise.

In his book *Reminiscences*, Boucher described the last time he saw Washington, during a brief encounter when the two chanced to meet while crossing the Potomac in the summer of 1775. Boucher warned Washington that the nation was headed for a "civil war" and that the colonists were on the downward path toward independence.

Washington thought not, and replied earnestly that "if ever I heard of his joining in any such measures I had his leave to set him down for everything wicked." Boucher formally ended his friendship with Washington in a bitter farewell letter, on August 6, 1775, in which he also caustically castigated the Whig cause.

In his sermons, Boucher could be equally vitriolic, but the arrogant loyalist often was more sound in his use of Scripture in behalf of the crown than were the Whigs who abused the Bible to justify armed revolt.

In 1775, in his parish church, St. Anne's, Boucher preached "Civil Liberty! Passive Obedience, and Non-Resistance," in response to a sermon preached and printed on the same topic by the Reverend Jacob Duché in Philadelphia (the turncoat minister still was backing the patriot cause at this point of his checkered career). Boucher had a penchant for using his messages as rebuttals to sermons with which he disagreed.

He chose as his text Galatians 5:1: "Stand fast therefore in the liberty wherewith Christ hath made us free . . ." The word *liberty* itself resonated within the breasts of patriots. They reveled in the fact the word was enshrined in Scripture. But Boucher knew, as the old, frayed saying goes, "a text taken out of context is pretext." He lashed out at those false ministers who put a political spin to a spiritual truth. "It has just been observed, that the liberty mendicated [sic] in the Scriptures, (and which alone the Apostle had in view in this text,) is wholly of the spiritual or religious kind. This liberty was the natural result of the new religion [Christian] in which mankind were then instructed; which certainly gave them no new civil privileges.

"They remained subject to the governments under which they lived, just as they had been before they became Christians, and just as others were who never became Christians; with this difference only, that the duty of submission and obedience to Government, was enjoined on converts to Christianity with new and stronger sanctions."

Abruptly dismissing any form of government based on "common consent" for the "common good," Boucher turned to another "notion not less popular, nor better founded." In this section Boucher spelled out his elitist views.

"This other notion is, that the whole human race is born equal; and that no man is naturally inferior, or, in any respect, subjected to another; and that he can be made subject to another only by his own consent. The position is equally ill-founded and false both in its premises and conclusions. In hardly any sense that can be imagined is the position strictly true but as applied to the case under consideration, it is demonstrably not true.

"Man differs from man on every thing that can be supposed to lead to supremacy and subjection, as one star differs from another star in glory . . . nor, without some relative inferiority and superiority, can there be any government."

Boucher's belief that all men were not born equal was out of step with the times, as shown by the soon-to-be signed Declaration of Independence, founded on this concept. But like many aristocratic loyalists, Boucher was convinced that only a minority usually supported revolutions, including the one in America. Such logic led him to conclude that this could result in government by "ignorant and corrupt tyrants." In a footnote in another sermon Boucher made an even stronger antiegalitarian argument, in the words of Dr. Falkner, a seventeenth-century divine:

But, to assert that the people, or inferiors, are, of right, judges of the cases in which they may resist their superiors, is as much to say, they are bound to subjection only as far as themselves shall think fit; and that they may claim an authority over their governors, and pass judgment upon them, and deprive them of their dignity, authority, and life itself, whensoever they shall think it requisite and needful.

Boucher warned rebellion violated the doctrine of nonresistance, which "is unquestionably a tenet of our Church." Switching from Scripture to the Thirty-nine Articles, the injunctions and homilies of the Anglican Church, Boucher quoted from the Church of England's formative documents:

> Lucifer was the first author and founder of rebellion; which is the first, the greatest, and the root of all other sins. King and princes, as well the evil as the good, do reign by God's ordinances; and subjects are bound to obey them, and for no cause to resist, or withstand, or rebel, or make any sedition against them, although they be wicked men. It were a perilous thing to commit unto subjects the judgment, which prince is wise, which government good; and which otherwise.
>
> A rebel is worse than the worst prince, and a rebellion worse than the worst government of the worst prince that hath hitherto been.

Jonathan Boucher's conservative principles had put him in a time warp. He asked for more than submission; he asked for servility. This was more than the spiritual descendants of Puritan Dissenters could swallow.

Boucher closed his sermon with an admonition from Scripture that outwardly seems to fly in the face of those superpatriots who had literally taken the law into their own hands:

> Submit yourselves to every ordinance of man, for the Lord's sake: whether it be to the king as supreme; or unto governors, as unto them that are sent by him for the punishment of evildoers, and for the praise of them that do well. For so is the

will of God, that with well doing ye may put to silence the
ignorance of foolish men: As free, and not using your liberty
for a cloke of maliciousness, but as the servants of God.
Honour all men. Love the brotherhood. Fear God. Honour
the king [1 Peter 2:13–17].

Was the American Revolution a really righteous rebellion,
despite the blessing given it by Puritan clergy? Did loyalist
Jonathan Boucher have a more correct view of Scripture than
Jonathan Mayhew?

The American Revolution was one of those wondrous
events in history from which multiple meanings can be drawn.
Dr. John K. Alexander, associate professor of history at the
University of Cincinnati, in a 1976 interview in the university's *Horizon* magazine, stated: "There were some noble
people fighting a noble war. There were also people who were
Loyalists, who opposed very much the American Revolution,
and who thought that all the statements about principles were
simply ridiculous, the bleatings of a bunch of agitators. There
were also a number of people who were neutral. It's a
complex matter."

The destructive aspects of the Revolution often get lost in
the glorification of our past. The Revolution dragged on for
seven years, leaving death, destruction, disease, and disloca-
tion of a large number of people in its wake.

Hundreds of young men left for Canada rather than fight in
what they considered to be an unjust rebellion. Out of a
population of fewer than 3 million, an estimated 100,000
Americans emigrated to Canada and England as political
refugees—including, of course, Jonathan Boucher. Their
property was confiscated.

In a provocative article asking, "Would Jesus Have Fought
for George Washington?" in the *U.S. Catholic Magazine* (July,

1976) Gordon C. Zahn argued that the Revolutionary War failed to meet the "just war" test in at least three respects: "The authority under which it was initiated and waged was, to put it most charitable, of highly doubtful legitimacy; the justice of the cause is open to serious question, and it was not a 'last resort.' "[10]

In the Declaration of Independence, Thomas Jefferson, attempting to win friends and influence people for the good of the cause, resorted to inflammatory rhetoric. He charged that King George had sunk to a state of "absolute Despotism" and "absolute Tyranny."

George III may have been politically inept to the point of being a bumbler, but he was far from being a tyrant. Walfred H. Peterson, professor of political science at Washington State University, has observed: "The real power in British government rested not with the king but with the Parliament, the cabinet and the prime minister. The king simply could not be a tyrant."[11] But the wily Jefferson knew that in a rebellion you need a scapegoat. And the fat king made an easy target.

American students are taught that "taxation without representation" was one of the major causes of the break with England. But do people really go to war over a tax on tea? As Boucher pointed out, three-fourths of the colonists at the time didn't even drink tea. But more to the point, applying biblical standards, was the complaint serious enough to justify violence?

"One suspects that Christ who once resolved a similar dilemma by checking the image on a tribute coin would not think so," Zahn stated. "Whose image is this? George III's?"

"Jesus *might* have been at Valley Forge," Zahn stated, "but only to relieve the suffering of men—just as he probably would have been found in the British and Hessian camps giving solace to lonely and confused men so far from home."

Does this then mean because the thirteen colonies used violence to achieve independence, we should be restrained from celebrating our freedom and love of country every July fourth? No—the Founding Fathers unleashed a set of political ideals that have stood the test of time and stirred the hearts of lovers of liberty around the world. These extraordinary men fashioned a nation that, despite its flaws, continues as a bastion of human rights and freedom in a world where those precious commodities are becoming increasingly rare.

As Zahn concluded in his essay, "God works in such wondrous, some times such wonderously devious, ways that even an unnecessary war of doubtful justice, fought under authority of dubious legitimacy could, and did, serve to open the way to a new vision of political freedom."

The spirit of '76 goes marching on!

AFTERMATH

Religion served as a handmaiden to the American Revolution. The War for Independence was truly a church-blessed war. But did the war return the favor?

Historians give different, even contradictory answers. J. Franklin Jameson described the fifteen-year period following the American Revolution as "the period of the lowest ebb-tide of vitality in the history of American Christianity."[1] Sydney Ahlstrom extends the period of spiritual malaise: "A colonial people almost congenitally exercised with religious questions of all sorts and possibly exhausted by or in reaction against the Great Awakening became preoccupied for forty years chiefly with the problems of politics."[2] Ahlstrom bolsters his argument with church membership figures, noting "not more than one person in twenty or possibly one in ten seems to have been affiliated" with a church.[3]

The exposure of American troops to Deism carried to these shores by French officers during the Revolution is credited or blamed for undermining the faith of many colonial believers. Indeed, historian Marion Starkey writes as if every French officer was a deistic evangelist who sat around the campfire trying to convert his American counterpart to the cult of reason, unimpeded by any language barrier.

"Boston [Congregationalism] had small cause to fear the papistry of the French," Starkey wrote. "The danger came from rationalism and Deism of many French officers. When the veterans came home at last, some would look at what went on in the old meetinghouse with fresh and skeptical eyes. Eventually, their skepticism would rend the Congregations asunder."[4]

If Deism was the new religion of the republic, then its foremost apostle was Thomas Paine "whose *Age of Reason* became one of the period's most famous [or infamous] exposition of deism."[5] The religious bulwarks set in place by the Great Awakening buckled like the walls of Jericho under Deism's onslaught on the campuses of Yale and Princeton. Lyman Beecher's 1795 report on God and man at Yale could have been written in 1988: "The College was in a most ungodly state. The college church was almost extinct. Most of the students were skeptical, and rowdies were plenty. Wine and liquor were kept in many rooms; intemperance, profanity, gambling, and licentiousness were common."[6] But if Yale was bad, Princeton was worse. Only two students in Princeton confessed to a belief in Christ!

The spiritual ravages of the war reached as far West as remote Logan County, Kentucky, which Peter Cartwright said "was called 'Rogue's Harbor' and was the refuge for escaped murderers, horse thieves, highway robbers and counterfeiters."[7]

What happened? Why did Americans march off to war as Christian soldiers only to return as skeptics? How could Deism not only thrive but prosper, as some historians assert, in the evangelical environment of New England?

A closer look, even in the writings of those who contend the faith of our fathers was impaled on the French sword of Deism, tells another story. Rationalism was not new to Puritan preachers. Bear in mind that most famous of evangelical Puritan preachers, Jonathan Edwards, who had a strong rationalistic streak. Even a cursory reading of his most celebrated philosophical treatise, "A Careful and Strict Enquiry into the modern prevailing Notions of that Freedom of Will, which is supposed to be essential to Moral Agency, Veture [sic] and Vice, Reward and Punishment, Praise and Blame," written in 1754, proves that point. Edwards, an intellectual giant and the scourge of the antirevivalist rationalist clergy, believed the mind, as well as the heart, was involved in a conversion experience.

Alan Heimert views the post-Revolutionary Enlightenment period more as an extension of the Awakening than do many other historians. But Heimert carefully explains the differences:

> It surely bears re-emphasis that the Enlightenment, as it came to America, was a far different faith from that of the pre-Revolutionary rationalist clergy. Indeed, it might even be argued that the American Enlightenment represented something of a translation into secular terms of the goals, and even the spirit, of the Awakening impulse. . . . Whatever the inner mechanism of the process, America's true Age of Reason unfolded, especially in its post-Revolutionary phase, more as a reaffirmation of evangelical principle than as a repudiation.[8]

Winthrop Hudson also argues that the threat that Deism would sweep Christianity into the dustbin of history was "more apparent than real. It is true that 'deistical societies' were formed and college students took delight in shocking their elders by calling each other Voltaire and Rousseau, but in retrospect it is clear that this 'radicalism' had no deep rootage."[9]

To at least one Puritan preacher, the winning of independence made the table level for all competing ideas and religions. In his Connecticut election sermon of 1783, Ezra Stiles accepted the challenge with relish: "Here [in America] Deism will have its full chance; nor need libertines [any] more to complain of being overcome by any weapons but the gentle, the powerful one of argument and truth. Revelation will be found to stand the test to the ten thousandth examination."[10]

From Sweet's *Story of Religion in America* one could also draw the conclusion that Deism was nipped in the bud before it could spread. Sweet used Lyman Beecher's account of the depraved condition at Yale College in 1795 as proof of the strong deistic influence sweeping across the land. Yet three pages later Sweet goes back to the same college in the same year to record one of the most profound spiritual turnarounds in recent history: "Timothy Dwight, the grandson of Jonathan Edwards, became the president in 1795, and under his administration the whole moral and religious atmosphere of the college was changed for the better. . . . Soon he had won the admiration of the students and in 1802 a revival began in which a third of the student body professed conversion, to be followed at frequent intervals at other awakenings."[11]

Whereas sin did abound in "Rogue's Harbor" in Logan County, Kentucky, grace did much more abound—in fact it would become the center of a revival meeting that would attract hundreds from miles around and would even spread to surrounding states. The first spark of the revival fires was reported in 1797, only fourteen years after the dismal report that Logan County was the spiritual cesspool of the West. In

Logan County at least, the "ebb tide of religion" soon gave way to a spiritual tidal wave.

Even the membership figures quoted by Sydney Ahlstrom as evidence religion fell on hard times immediately after the close of the war may be misleading. Standards for church membership vary greatly within denominations and from one century to the next. In seventeenth-century New England, one had to prove one had been "elected" through a religious experience before one could claim the covenant and become a member of the church. Contrast that with the comparative ease of joining a church in most mainstream denominations today and one can understand why 72 percent of Americans believe they have a good to excellent chance of going to heaven.[12] But it is patently obvious that comfortable assumption is not as biblically based as the beliefs of the Puritans, who spent a great deal of their time tossing and turning on their "iron couches of introspection."

Though the Revolution may not have had as deep an impact on religious beliefs as is commonly believed, the war *did* affect the institutional church. When the war began, nine of the thirteen colonies had their own established churches. The Church of England prevailed in states as far north as New York and as far south as Georgia. Congregationalism was established in Massachusetts, Connecticut, and New Hampshire. Ironically, Massachusetts, where the first shots for liberty were fired, was the last colony to disestablish the Congregationalist Church, in 1833.

Though the war left the British-backed Anglican church in ruins, political liberty translated into complete religious freedom for more evangelical dissenting groups such as Baptists and Methodists. Both rode the crest of the waves of the westward migration. Congregationalists, however, could never get the intellectual faith of their fathers to spread as quickly among the families on the frontier.

The changes wrought in the two established denominations—Anglicanism and Congregationalism—and in two independent communions—Baptists and Methodists—by the winds of war will help answer the question of how the churches in general fared in post-Revolution America.

Ironically Congregationalists who came to these shores as religious dissenters settled in and became the religious establishment. Puritans had left England so they could worship their own way, not to establish religious freedom; unlike us, they did not venerate democracy. However, their own principles of church polity—ordaining their own pastors, electing their own church officers, embracing the idea of the sovereignty of the people—undermined the Puritans. In time these radical beliefs would permeate both the political and religious realms and the Congregationalists would lose their privileged status in Massachusetts.

At the outset of the war, the Congregational church had been the largest, the richest, and the most influential of all the colonial churches; its members also had the best education.[13] One could likewise argue that the Congregationalists invented the word *independence*. Most of the Massachusetts war hawks occupied Congregationalist pews on Sunday. But independence is a two-edged sword. "Close reasoning" on religious and political issues, so valued by Congregationalists, finally evolved into freethinking and led to Unitarianism.

Actually, Congregationalists fought an internal war on two fronts—the revivalists versus the antirevivalists and the traditional Calvinists versus the radical Arminians. Still, the internal struggles within their congregations did not prevent them from joining the Presbyterians in one of the first denominational mergers in America, in 1801. The agreement permitted new churches on the frontier to call a minister from either denomination. Unfortunately for the Congregationalists, the plan favored the Presbyterians, who remained determined to maintain their own identity.

Although the Congregationalists and Presbyterians could not keep pace with the Baptists or Methodists in recruiting members, the spiritual heirs of Jonathan Edwards and John Witherspoon did make "the largest contributions to the educational and cultural life of the frontier."[14] They were the first to establish schools and colleges on the western frontier, as they had in the "howling wilderness" of Massachusetts in the early seventeenth century.

What of the other established church? A devout Episcopalian had to walk a narrow line during the Revolution or face the possibility of being tarred and feathered or even suffering the loss of property—or both. Members of the Church of England, especially in New England, became aliens in their own country; and Anglicans usually had more property to lose than members of less prestigious communions.

Even in Virginia, where Washington, Jefferson, and Madison attended Anglican services, the Episcopal Church could not escape the fury of Whig hatred. "At the opening of the war in Virginia there were 95 parishes, 164 churches and chapels and 91 clergymen. When the war closed 23 of the 95 parishes were either forsaken or extinct and of the remainder only 34 had ministers."[15] During the war, the Episcopal Church lost seventy thousand members, who emigrated to Canada to escape persecution. In the South Methodists, who still remained within Anglicanism, seceded from the denomination to join the Whig cause or at least to remain neutral.

In the Episcopal Church, priests are ordained by the laying on of hands by the bishops. But the cry "no king, no bishop" had prevented the Church of England from posting a bishop in America both before and during the Revolution. With a depleted ministry and no on-site bishop, in 1783 it did indeed look as if the Anglican Church would "die out with the old families."[16]

The problem was solved by subterfuge. Ten Connecticut Anglican priests met secretly to select the first Anglican bishop in the United States. The lot fell to Samuel Seabury, a fire-breathing Tory and erstwhile chaplain to British troops. Unable to obtain consecration in England, the persistent Seabury traveled to Scotland, where three "Jacobite" bishops—clergy who remained loyal to the heirs of James II—laid hands on him in November of 1784. Seabury returned home and performed his priestly functions without interference or intimidation.[17] The Protestant Episcopal Church met for its first General Convention in 1789, but it took it an entire generation for the reconstituted Episcopalians to recover from the wounds of war.

The Methodist Episcopal Church, a branch broken off the Anglican tree, survived under duress during the Revolution and after the war put other denominations in the shade with its spread throughout the South and West. "The Revolutionary War now being closed and a general peace being established," wrote Jesse Lee, the first official historian of Methodism, "we could go into all parts of the country without fear; and we soon began to enlarge our borders and to preach in many places where we had not been before."[18] By 1820 the fast-growing Methodists had eclipsed the Baptists as the largest American denomination.

Methodists began as a "religious society" in a somewhat tenuous connection with the Anglican Church. John Wesley, Methodism's founder, was an ordained Anglican priest who never left the Church of England. But Wesley's outspoken opposition to independence caused Whig militants to eye the 15,000 Americans who called themselves Methodists with suspicion. With the exception of Francis Asbury, all Wesley's lay preachers left the country during the Revolution. The outlook for the fledgling communion seemed so bleak that a spectator watching a Methodist chapel being built in Delaware during the war sarcastically commented: "It's no use putting up so large a dwelling for Methodists, for after the war a corncrib will hold them all."[19]

But the Methodists had a secret weapon and an evangelistic strategy that seemed divinely inspired to meet the spiritual needs of a postwar nation on the move. Circuit riders followed the westward movement, making converts and then organizing them into "class meetings" shepherded by local lay preachers and class leaders.

John Wesley was a genius when it came to organization. The circuit system was transplanted to America from England, where Wesley had organized his followers into societies that were visited regularly by Wesley's ordained "Mounties." Prior to the Revolution, because of the lack of an ordained ministry, American Methodists had depended on Anglican priests to administer the sacraments of baptism and the Lord's Supper. The ever-practical Wesley solved the problem with a little ecclesiastical fudging. Searching the Scriptures and church history, Wesley decided that "Ordination by presbyters was valid when dictated by necessity, and he found justification for it in the practice of the ancient church at Alexandria where presbyters had even ordained bishops."[20]

Wesley ordained three men in England, who returned home in time to ordain Francis Asbury as deacon, elder, and superintendent at the Christmas Conference, in 1784, in Baltimore. Thus the new American Methodist Church was born just in time to grow with a new nation. By the middle of the next century, the warm evangelical Methodists had captured the hearts of Middle America.

Baptists revel in being the chief of dissenters among American churches. As strict state-church separatists, the Baptists have relied more on evangelism than governmental favors for adding to their church rolls. As a result of the Separates, who left the established denominations to join the Baptist ranks, the Baptists did well prior to and during the Revolution. They did even better after the Revolution, when the states cut their bonds with the established churches.

The Baptists' evangelistic zeal and emphasis on Scripture carried the denomination to the top in recruiting members among the "three old denominations" (Presbyterians and Congregationalists were the other two) of English dissent by 1800 "with twice as many adherents as any other religious group."[21]

With its Bible-believing stance, the Baptist church did well among the backwoods folk in the West but gained even more members among the seaboard states in the East and South. Contrary to public opinion, Baptist preachers were not unlearned Bible thumpers, "As Baptists multiplied in the closing decades of the eighteenth century, they were busy with projects for establishing academies and a college."[22]

For the good of all American denominations, Baptists played a key roll with their persistent agitation for cutting the ties that bound churches to the state. Throughout the Revolution, Baptists continued to fight to disestablish the Congregationalist Church in Massachusetts, but to no avail. The church was too deeply embedded in the political structure of the Commonwealth for them to so easily dislodge it. Besides, most Whig patriots in Massachusetts were convinced Congregationalists.

In contrast, establishment did not work to the advantage of the Anglican Church in Virginia. The majority of Whigs viewed the Anglican Church as a clerical hothouse of Loyalist traitors. Although some of the best-known names in the American Revolution—Washington, Jefferson, and Madison—attended Anglican services in Virginia, one wonders whether they prayed or plotted in church. Madison and Jefferson, of course, played pivotal roles in establishing religious equality in the Old Dominion.

After the Revolution, Baptists continued to lobby for religious freedom in Virginia, but their efforts were nearly sidelined in 1784. On the face of things, a compromise bill, permitting the citizens to earmark their tax assessment for the church of their choice, sounded good. Some Presbyterian clergy even endorsed it. But the Baptists stood firm in their opposition. They did not want any tax money going to support any church—established or otherwise. The Baptists declared it "to be repugnant to the spirit of the Gospel for the Legislature thus to proceed in matters of religion, that no human laws ought to be established for this purpose."[23]

Thomas Jefferson's freedom-of-religion measure was finally passed by the Virginia Legislature in 1785. Later the concept would be incorporated into the Bill of Rights as an important component of the First Amendment to the Constitution. To make sure the world would never forget the role he played in promoting a basic fundamental right, Jefferson put in writing the fact that he was the author of the "Statute of Virginia for Religious Freedom" on his tombstone.

However, Jefferson may have gotten more credit than he deserves. William Warren Sweet argues: "Justice compels the admission that Jefferson's part in this accomplishment was not so great as that of James Madison, nor were the contributions of either or both as important as was that of the humble people called Baptists."[24]

In one of the paradoxes of the alliance between evangelical religion and politics in the American Revolution, conservative theology did not necessarily beget conservative political offspring. The most radical political patriots—Sam Adams and Patrick Henry—were theological conservatives. Yet evangelical Methodists and Baptists felt far more at home in the political pew with Thomas Jefferson—who had embraced the cult of reason over revealed religion—than with liberal Congregationalists, who were political conservatives, as typified by John Adams.

Not all defenders of Deism came from foreign shores. Ethan Allen, hero of Ticonderoga and a self-educated rebel from the Great Awakening, published his *The Only Oracle of Man* in 1784—one year after the Treaty of Paris. Allen not only defended "natural religion" but attacked the Bible and "priestcraft" with such boldness that the work was regarded as "the first formal publication, in the United States, openly directed against the Christian religion."[25]

Thomas Paine, who had fired the colonies to take up arms against the British with his *Common Sense*, now produced his ode to Deism, *Age of Reason*.

Staunch republican Sam Adams, who had linked arms with Paine to promote revolution, found Paine's infidelism too much for his stomach. In a letter written at Boston, and dated November 30, 1802, Adams began his letter to Paine with "Sir" and ended it with "Adieu" after castigating his old friend for his "defense of infidelity." "Do you think that your pen, or the pen of any other man, can unchristianize the mass of our citizens, or have you hopes of converting a few to assist you in so bad a cause?" he asked. "The people of New

England, if you will allow me to use a Scripture phrase, are fast returning to their first love."

In one of the important books of this decade, *The Naked Public Square*, Richard John Neuhaus makes the point:

> The American experiment, which, more than any other, has been normative for the world's thinking about democracy, is not only derived from religiously grounded belief, it continues to depend upon such belief. In his first year as vice president under the new constitution, John Adams said: "We have no government armed with power capable of contending with human passions unbridled by morality and religion. Our constitution was made only for a moral and religious people. It is wholly inadequate for the government of any other."[26]

Neuhaus further states: "The assertion that we have 'moved beyond' the possibility of a religious grounding of democracy says more about those who make the assertion than it does about American society. Americans, as a people, are as religious, probably more religious, than they have ever been."[27]

Neuhaus's astute observations of modern America and the role of religion in our society reflect the sentiments of an equally incisive observer from France. More than 150 years ago, Alexis de Tocqueville wrote:

> The religious atmosphere of the country was the first thing that struck me on arrival in the United States. The longer I stayed in the country, the more conscious I became of the important political consequences resulting from this novel situation.
>
> In France I had seen the spirits of religion and of freedom almost always marching in opposite directions. In America I found them intimately linked together in joint reign over the same land.[28]

Religion, which never intervenes directly in the government of American society, should therefore be considered as the first of their political institutions, for although it did not give them the taste for liberty, it singularly facilitates their use thereof.

The inhabitants of the United States themselves consider religious beliefs from this angle. I do not know if all Americans have faith in their religion—for who can read the secrets of the heart?—but I am sure that they think it necessary to the maintenance of republican institutions. That is not the view of one class or party among the citizens, but of the whole nation; it is found in all ranks.[29]

SOURCE NOTES

Introduction

1. George Washington, "Farewell Address" (Washington, D.C.: Liberty Lobby Pamphlet).
2. Peter J. Ferara, *Religion and the Constitution: A Reinterpretation* (Washington, D.C.: Free Congress Foundation, 1983).
3. Ibid.

Chapter 1

1. J. T. Headley, *The Chaplains and Clergy of the Revolution* (New York: Charles Scribner, 1864), 75.
2. Editors of American Heritage, *The American Heritage Book of the Revolution* (New York: American Heritage Publishing Co., 1971), 100.
3. Stewart Beach, *Samuel Adams: The Fateful Years 1764–1776* (New York: Dodd, Mead & Company, 1965), 279.
4. Donald Barr Chidsey, *The World of Samuel Adams* (Nashville, Tenn.: Thomas Nelson, 1974), 176.
5. Headley, *Chaplains and Clergy*, 76.
6. Ibid.
7. Ibid. Italics added.
8. Ibid.
9. Alice M. Baldwin, *The New England Clergy and the American Revolution* (Durham, N.C.: Duke University Press, 1928), 95.
10. Ibid.
11. Ibid., 138.

12. Ibid., 180.

13. Edmund Burke, *On the American Revolution, Selected Speeches and Letters* (New York: Harper Torchbooks / Harper & Row Publishers, 1966), 86.

14. Gordon S. Wood, *Creation of the American Republic* (Chapel Hill, N.C.: University of North Carolina Press, 1969), 3.

15. John Wingate Thornton, *The Pulpit of the American Revolution* (New York: Burt Franklin, 1970), xxxviii.

Chapter 2

1. Carl Bridenbaugh, *Mitre and Sceptre* (New York: Oxford University Press, 1962), 190.

2. Alice M. Baldwin, *The New England Clergy and the American Revolution* (Durham, N.C.: Duke University Press, 1928), 4.

3. William Buell Sprague, *Annals of the American Pulpit*, vol. 2 (New York: R. Carter & Bros., 1817), 48.

4. Arthur M. Schlesinger, *The Birth of a Nation* (New York: Alfred A. Knopf, 1968), 73.

5. Ibid., 84.

6. Ibid.

7. James Truslow Adams, *Revolutionary New England, 1691–1776* (Boston: Atlantic Monthly Press, 1923), 33.

8. Schlesinger, *Birth*, 84.

9. Sydney E. Ahlstrom, *A Religious History of the American People* (New Haven, Conn.: Yale University Press, 1972), 124.

10. Patricia U. Bonomi, *Under the Cope of Heaven: Religion, Society, and Politics in Colonial America* (New York: Oxford University Press, 1986), 221.

11. Ibid.

12. Alexis de Tocqueville, *Democracy in America*, trans. George Lawrence, ed. J. P. Mayer and Max Lerner (New York: Harper & Row, 1966), 268.

13. Carl Bridenbaugh, *Mitre and Sceptre* (New York: Oxford University Press, 1962), xi.

14. Ibid., xiv.

15. Bridenbaugh, *Mitre and Sceptre*, 189.
16. Alice M. Baldwin, *New England Clergy*, xii.
17. Bridenbaugh, *Mitre*, 192.
18. Ibid., 191.
19. Ibid., 190.
20. John Wingate Thornton, *The Pulpit of the American Revolution* (New York: Burt Franklin, 1970), xxvi.
21. Baldwin, *New England Clergy*, 6, quoting J. Winsor, *Memorial History of Boston*.
22. Philip Davidson, *Propaganda and the American Revolution* (Chapel Hill, N.C.: University of North Carolina Press, 1941), 95.
23. Ibid.
24. Bridenbaugh, *Mitre*, 190–191.
25. Peter Oliver, *The Origin and Progress of the American Rebellion*, ed. Douglass Adair and John A. Schutz (San Marino, Calif.: Huntington Library, 1961), 42.
26. Carol Berkin, *Jonathan Sewall, Odyssey of an American Loyalist* (New York: Columbia University Press, 1974), 113. Italics added.
27. Thornton, *Pulpit*, xxix.

Chapter 3

1. Claude H. Van Tyne, *The Causes of the War of Independence* (Boston: Houghton Mifflin Co., 1922), 5.
2. George F. Willison's introduction to William Bradford, *The History of Plymouth Colony* (Roslyn, N.Y.: Walter J. Black, 1948), ix.
3. Marion L. Starkey, *The Congregational Way* (New York: Doubleday & Co., 1966), 10.
4. Will Durant, *The Reformation*, vol. 6 in *The Story of Civilization* (New York: Simon & Schuster, 1957), 37.
5. Willison, *Plymouth Colony*, xi.
6. Durant, *Reformation*, 596.
7. Clifton E. Olmstead, *History of Religion in the United States* (Englewood Cliffs, N.J.: Prentice-Hall, 1960), 63.
8. William Warren Sweet, *Religion in Colonial America* (New York: Charles Scribner's Sons, 1942), 16.

9. Sweet, *Colonial America*, 20.

10. Willison, *Plymouth Colony*, xi.

11. Samuel Eliot Morison, *The Oxford History of the American People* (New York: Oxford University Press, 1965), 55.

12. Charles M. Andrews, *The Settlements of New Haven*, vol. 4 in *The Colonial Period of American History* (New Haven, Conn.: Yale University Press, 1964), 395.

13. Willison, *Plymouth Colony*, viii.

14. Van Tyne, *War of Independence*, 3.

15. Ibid., 3.

16. Sweet, *Colonial America*, 18.

Chapter 4

1. Marion L. Starkey, *The Congregational Way* (New York: Doubleday & Co., 1966), 48–49.

2. Perry Miller, *Errand Into the Wilderness* (Cambridge, Mass.: Belknap Press, 1956), 5.

3. John Winthrop, "A Modell of Christian Charity," *The Annals of America*, vol. 1., "Discovering a New World" (Chicago: Encyclopedia Britannica, 1968), 115.

4. Ibid.

5. Miller, *Errand*, 5.

6. Ibid.

7. William Warren Sweet, *The Story of Religion in America* (New York: Harper & Bros., 1950), 51.

8. Winthrop, "A Modell," 115.

9. Ibid.

10. Sweet, *Religion in Colonial America* (New York: Charles Scribner's Sons, 1942), 188. Quoting from the Colonial Records, vol. 1, 87.

11. Ibid., 87.

12. Miller, *Errand*, 162.

13. Perry Miller, *Nature's Nation* (Cambridge, Mass.: Belknap Press, 1967), 17–18.

14. Sweet, *Colonial America*, footnote, 88.

15. Miller, *Errand*, 11.

16. Ibid.
17. Ibid., 14.
18. Ibid., 15.
19. Ibid.
20. Starkey, *Congregational Way*, 49.
21. Miller, *Errand*, 11.

Chapter 5

1. Sydney E. Ahlstrom, *A Religious History of the American People* (New Haven, Conn.: Yale University Press, 1972), 129.
2. William Warren Sweet, *The Story of Religion in America* (New York: Harper & Bros., 1950), 46–47.
3. Ibid., 57–58.
4. Ahlstrom, *Religious History*, 148.
5. Ibid., 149.
6. William Warren Sweet, *Religion in Colonial America* (New York: Charles Scribner's Sons, 1942), 101.
7. Perry Miller, *Religion in Nature's Nation* (Cambridge, Mass.: Belknap Press, 1967), 26.
8. Marion L. Starkey, *The Congregational Way* (New York: Doubleday & Co., 1966), 96.
9. G. Adolph Koch, *Republican Religion: The American Revolution and the Cult of Reason* (New York: Henry Holt, 1933), 6.
10. Ibid., 7.
11. Starkey, *Congregational Way*, 150.
12. Sweet, *Story of Religion*, 60.
13. Ibid., 61.
14. Ibid.
15. Ibid., 65

Chapter 6

1. Carl Bridenbaugh, *Mitre and Sceptre* (New York: Oxford University Press, 1962), 201.
2. John Wingate Thornton, *The Pulpit of the American Revolution* (New York: Burt Franklin, 1970), 44.

3. Moses Coit Tyler, *The Literary History of the American Revolution* (New York: Barnes & Noble, 1897), 125.

4. Ibid., 128.

5. Ibid., 122.

6. Ibid., 124.

7. Ibid., 129.

8. Ibid.

9. Ibid. Italics added.

10. Alice M. Baldwin, *The New England Clergy and the American Revolution* (Durham, N.C.: Duke University Press, 1928), 172.

11. Bridenbaugh, *Mitre and Sceptre*, 240.

12. Claude H. Van Tyne, *The Causes of the War of Independence* (Boston and New York: Houghton Mifflin Co., 1922), 358.

13. Thornton, *Pulpit*, 51.

14. Ibid., 43.

15. Bridenbaugh, *Mitre and Sceptre*, 100.

16. Thornton, *Pulpit*, 43.

17. Ibid., 42.

18. All references to Mayhew's sermon, "Discourse Concerning Unlimited Submission and Non-Resistance to the Higher Powers," from Thornton, *Pulpit*, 47–104. Italics added.

19. Perry Miller, *Errand Into the Wilderness* (Cambridge, Mass.: Belknap Press, 1956), 152.

20. Ibid.

21. Bridenbaugh, *Mitre*, 102. Italics added.

Chapter 7

1. Bernhard Knollenberg, *Origins of the American Revolution, 1759–1766* (New York: Macmillan, 1960), 70.

2. Donald Barr Chidsey, *The World of Samuel Adams* (Nashville, Tenn.: Thomas Nelson, 1974), 124.

3. John Wingate Thornton, *The Pulpit of the American Revolution* (New York: Burt Franklin, 1970), 44–45. Italics added.

4. Carl Bridenbaugh, *Mitre and Sceptre* (New York: Oxford University Press, 1962), 204.

5. Chidsey, *Samuel Adams*, 65.

6. Moses Coit Tyler, *The Literary History of the American Revolution* (New York: Barnes & Noble, 1897), 139.

7. Ibid., 44–45.

8. Chidsey, *Samuel Adams*, 65.

9. Quotations from Mayhew's sermon, "Discourse Concerning Unlimited Submission and Non-Resistance to the Higher Powers," from Thornton, *Pulpit*, 87. Italics added.

10. Alice M. Baldwin, *The New England Clergy and the American Revolution* (Durham, N.C.: Duke University Press, 1928), 170.

Chapter 8

1. Edmund Burke, *Burke on the American Revolution*, ed. Elliott Robert Barkan (New York: Harper & Row, 1966), 82–84.

2. Claude H. Van Tyne, *England & America: Rivals in the American Revolution* (New York: Macmillan Co., 1927), 68.

3. Ibid.

4. Ibid.

5. Ibid.

6. John Adams, *Works of John Adams*, vol. 10 (Boston: Little, Brown & Co., 1850–1856), 85.

7. John Wingate Thornton, *The Pulpit of the American Revolution* (New York: Burt Franklin, 1860), xxx.

8. Carl Bridenbaugh, *Mitre and Sceptre* (New York: Oxford University Press, 1962), 256.

9. Ibid., 256.

10. Ibid., 257.

11. Ibid.

12. Ibid., 256. Italics added.

13. Ibid., 257.

14. Quoted from C. S. Lewis's introduction to J. B. Phillips, *Letters to Young Churches* (New York: Macmillan Co., 1967), x.

15. Bernard Bailyn, *The Ideological Origins of the American Revolution* (Cambridge, Mass.: Belknap Press, 1965), 95.

16. Bridenbaugh, *Mitre*, 218.

17. Alan Heimert, *Religion and the American Mind From the Great Awakening to the American Revolution* (Cambridge, Mass.: Harvard University Press, 1966), 362.

18. Bailyn, *Origins*, 96.

19. Edwin Scott Gaustad, *A Religious History of America* (New York: Harper & Row, 1966), 77.

20. Bridenbaugh, *Mitre*, 244.

21. Ibid., 245.

22. Ibid., 323.

23. Ibid., 312.

24. Arthur Lyon Cross, *The Anglican Episcopate and the American Colonies* (New York: Longmans, Green & Co., 1902), 270–271.

25. Van Tyne, *War of Independence*, 354–355.

26. Bridenbaugh, *Mitre*, 313.

Chapter 9

1. Alan Heimert, *Religion and the American Mind From the Great Awakening to the American Revolution* (Cambridge, Mass.: Harvard University Press, 1966), 140.

2. Ibid., 17.

3. William Warren Sweet, *Religion in Colonial America* (New York: Charles Scribner's Sons, 1942), 273.

4. Heimert, *Religion and the American Mind*, 12.

5. Ibid., 21. Yale's Sydney Ahlstrom argues that Harvard's Alan Heimert placed too much weight on the religious influence of the Revolution. Historians are divided on the issue, but Heimert's important book helps offset many other historians who seldom give religion a fair hearing when they trace the origins of the conflict.

6. Ibid., 56.

7. Ibid., 96

8. Heimert, *Religion and the American Mind*, 98.

9. Winthrop S. Hudson, *Religion in America* (New York: Charles Scribner's Sons, 1981), 65.

10. James Truslow Adams, *Revolutionary New England, 1691–1776* (Boston: Atlantic Monthly Press, 1923), 170.

11. Sydney E. Ahlstrom, *A Religious History of the American People* (New Haven, Conn.: Yale University Press, 1972), 301.

12. William Warren Sweet, *The Story of Religion in America* (New York: Harper & Bros., 1950), 129.

13. Ibid., 130.

14. Ahlstrom, *Religious History*, 282.

15. Ibid., 302.

16. Ahlstrom, *Religious History*, 299.

17. Arthur M. Schlesinger, *The Birth of the Nation* (New York: Alfred A. Knopf, 1968), 87.

18. Ahlstrom, *Religious History*, 303.

19. Ibid.

20. Ibid.

21. Hudson, *Religion in America*, 65.

22. Ahlstrom, *Religious History*, 306.

23. Heimert, *Religion and the American Mind*, 13.

24. Ibid., 14.

25. Ibid., 12.

26. Perry Miller, *Errand Into the Wilderness* (Cambridge, Mass.: Belknap Press, 1956), 162.

27. Ibid., 163.

28. Heimert, *Religion and the American Mind*, 396.

29. Miller, *Errand*, 164.

30. Ibid.

31. Ibid., 165. Italics added.

32. Heimert, *Religion and the American Mind*, 302.

33. Edwin Scott Gaustad, *A Religious History of America* (New York: Harper & Row, 1966), 98.

34. John Pollack, *George Whitefield and the Great Awakening* (New York: Doubleday, 1972), 162.

35. Ahlstrom, *Religious History*, 290.

36. Ibid., 294.

37. Schlesinger, *Birth*, 93.

38. Ahlstrom, *Religious History*, 294.

39. Heimert, *Religion and the American Mind*, 12.

40. Ahlstrom, *Religious History*, 350.

Chapter 10

1. All quotations from Samuel Langdon's sermon are from John Wingate Thornton, *The Pulpit of the American Revolution* (New York: Burt Franklin, 1970), 233, containing its full text.
2. Moses Coit Tyler, *The Literary History of the American Revolution 1763–1783*, vol. 2 (New York: G. P. Putnam's Sons, 1900), 17.
3. J. T. Headley, *Chaplains and Clergy of the Revolution* (New York: Charles Scribner, 1864).
4. Mark A. Noll, *The Search for Christian America* (Westchester, Ill.: Crossway Books, 1983), 64–65.

Chapter 11

1. John Wingate Thornton, *The Pulpit of the American Revolution* (New York: Burt Franklin, 1970), 261. Italics added.
2. Ibid.
3. Editors of American Heritage, *The American Heritage Book of the Revolution* (New York: American Heritage Publishing Co., 1971), 109.
4. Quotations from Samuel West's sermon are from John Wingate Thornton, *The Pulpit of the American Revolution* (New York: Burt Franklin, 1970). Italics added.

Chapter 12

1. For the portraits of these brave chaplains and clergy who served in the Revolution, I am indebted to J. T. Headley, *Chaplains and Clergy of the Revolution* (New York: Charles Scribner, 1864), from which I have selected the most interesting and colorful individuals. All quotations in this chapter are from Headley's volume.

Chapter 13

1. All quotations from Peter Oliver are from Peter Oliver, *Peter Oliver's Origin and Progress of the American Rebellion*, ed. Douglass

Adair and John A. Schutz (San Marino, Calif.: Huntington Library, 1961), vii. Italics added.

2. Carl Bridenbaugh, *Mitre and Sceptre* (New York: Oxford University Press, 1962), xiv.

3. Oliver, *Origin and Progress*, xv.

4. Ibid., x.

5. Ibid., xi.

6. Anne Y. Zimmer, *Jonathan Boucher: Loyalist in Exile* (Detroit: Wayne State University, 1978), 161.

7. All quotations from Jonathan Boucher, ibid.

8. Ibid., 269.

9. Gordon Zahn, "Would Jesus Have Fought for George Washington?" *U.S. Catholic Magazine* (July 1976), 6.

10. "Would You Have Signed the Declaration of Independence?" *Eternity* (July 1971), 19.

Aftermath

1. William Warren Sweet, *The Story of Religion in America* (New York: Harper & Bros., 1950), 233, quoting J. Franklin Jameson, *The American Revolution Considered as a Social Movement* (Princeton, 1926), 148.

2. Sydney Ahlstrom, *A Religious History of the American People* (New Haven, Conn.: Yale University Press, 1972), 365.

3. Ibid.

4. Marion L. Starkey, *The Congregational Way* (New York: Doubleday & Co., 1966), 165.

5. Ahlstrom, *Religious History*, 367.

6. Sweet, *Story of Religion*, 223–224.

7. Ibid., 225.

8. Alan Heimert, *Religion and the American Mind From the Great Awakening to the Revolution* (Cambridge, Mass.: Harvard University Press, 1966), 538.

9. Winthrop S. Hudson, *Religion in America* (New York: Charles Scribner's Sons, 1981), 132.

10. John Wingate Thornton, *The Pulpit of the American Revolution* (New York: Burt Franklin, 1970), 471.

11. Sweet, *Story of Religion*, 226.

12. "We Believe—and We Believe We're Going to Heaven," *U.S.A. Weekend* (December 19, 1986), 4.

13. Hudson, *Religion in America*, 118.

14. Sweet, *Story of Religion*, 214.

15. Ibid., 195.

16. Hudson, *Religion in America*, 116.

17. Ahlstrom, *Religious History*, 369.

18. Hudson, *Religion in America*, 123, quoting *Short History of Methodism* (Baltimore, 1910), 84.

19. Ibid., 122, quoting from J. M. Buckley, *A History of Methodists in the United States* (New York, 1896), 186.

20. Ibid., 123.

21. Ibid., 121.

22. Ibid., 122.

23. Sweet, *Story of Religion*, 192.

24. Ibid., 193.

25. Ahlstrom, *Religious History*, 367.

26. Richard John Neuhaus, *The Naked Public Square* (Grand Rapids, Mich.: W. B. Eerdmans Publishing Co., 1984), 95.

27. Ibid.

28. Alexis de Tocqueville, *Democracy in America*, trans. George Lawrence, ed. J. P. Mayer and Max Lerner (New York: Harper & Row, 1966), 271–272.

29. Ibid., 269.

SELECTED
BIBLIOGRAPHY

Adams, James Truslow. *Revolutionary New England, 1691–1776.* Boston: Atlantic Monthly Press, 1923.

Adams, John. *Works of John Adams.* Boston: Little, Brown & Co., 1850–56.

Ahlstrom, Sydney E. *A Religious History of the American People.* New Haven, Conn.: Yale University Press, 1972.

Bailyn, Bernard. *The Ideological Origins of the American Revolution.* Cambridge, Mass.: Belknap Press, 1965.

Baldwin, Alice M. *The New England Clergy and the American Revolution.* Durham, N.C.: Duke University Press, 1928.

Berkin, Carol. *Jonathan Sewell, Odyssey of an American Loyalist.* New York: Columbia University Press, 1974.

Boatner, Mark M. *Landmarks of the American Revolution.* Hawthorne Books, 1975.

Boucher, Jonathan. *A View of the Causes and Consequences of the American Revolution in Thirteen Discourses.* London: G. G. & J. Robinson, 1797.

Bridenbaugh, Carl. *Mitre and Sceptre.* New York: Oxford University Press, 1962.

Chidsey, Donald Barr. *The World of Samuel Adams*. Nashville, Tenn.: Thomas Nelson, Inc., 1974.

Cross, Arthur Lyon. *The Anglican Episcopate and the American Colonies*. New York: Longmans, Green & Co., 1902.

Davidson, Philip. *Propaganda and the American Revolution*. Durham, N.C.: University of North Carolina Press, 1941.

Editors of American Heritage. *The American Heritage Book of the Revolution*. New York: American Heritage Pub. Co., 1958.

Edwards, George R. *Jesus and the Politics of Violence*. New York: Harper & Row, 1972.

Gaustad, Edwin Scott. *A Religious History of America*. New York: Harper & Row, 1966.

Gingerich, Melvin. *The Christian and Revolution*. Scottdale, Pa.: Herald Press, 1968.

Gipson, Lawrence Henry. *The Coming of the Revolution, 1763–1775*. New York: Harper Torchbooks, 1954.

Headley, J. T. *Chaplains and Clergy of the Revolution*. New York: Charles Scribner, 1864.

Heimert, Alan. *Religion and the American Mind From the Great Awakening to the Revolution*. Cambridge, Mass.: Harvard University Press, 1966.

Hill, Christopher. *Society and Puritanism in Pre-Revolutionary England*. New York: Schocken Books, 1964.

Hitt, Russell, ed. *Heroic Colonial Christians*. New York: Lippincott Co., 1966.

Hudson, Winthrop S. *Nationalism and Religion in America*. New York: Harper & Row, 1970.

Hudson, Winthrop S. *Religion in America*. New York: Charles Scribner's Sons, 1965.

Jones, Howard Mumford and Bessie Zaban. *The Many Voices of Boston*. Boston: Little, Brown & Co., 1975.

Ketcham, Ralph. *From Colony to Country: the Revolution in American Thought, 1750–1820*. New York: Macmillan Publishing Corp., 1974.

Knollenberg, Bernard. *Origin of the American Revolution, 1759–1766.* New York: Macmillan Co., 1960.

Lewy, Guenter. *Religion and Revolution.* New York: Oxford University Press, 1974.

Metzger, Charles H. *Catholics and the American Revolution.* Chicago: Loyola University Press, 1962.

Miller, John C. *Origins of the American Revolution.* Boston: Little, Brown & Co., 1943.

Miller, Perry. *Edwards.* William Sloane Associated, 1949.

Miller, Perry. *Errand Into the Wilderness.* Cambridge, Mass.: Belknap Press, 1956.

Miller, Perry. *Nature's Nation.* Cambridge, Mass.: Belknap Press, 1967.

Morgan, Edmund S. *The Birth of the Republic, 1763–89.* Chicago: University of Chicago Press, 1956.

Oliver, Peter. *Peter Oliver's Origin and Progress of the American Rebellion.* Edited by Douglass Adair and John A. Schutz. San Marino, Calif.: Huntington Library, 1961.

Olmstead, Clifton E. *History of Religion in the United States.* Englewood Cliffs, N.J.: Prentice-Hall, 1960.

Schlesinger, Arthur M. *The Birth of the Nation.* New York: Alfred A. Knopf, 1968.

Sprague, William Buell. *Annals of the American Pulpit.* New York: R. Carter and Brothers, 1817.

Starkey, Marion L. *The Congregational Way.* New York: Doubleday & Co., 1966.

Sweet, William Warren. *The Story of Religion in America.* New York: Charles Scribner's Sons, 1939.

Sweet, William Warren. *Religion in Colonial America.* New York: Charles Scribner's Sons, 1942.

Thornton, John Wingate. *The Pulpit of the American Revolution.* New York: Burt Franklin, 1970.

Tyler, Moses Coit. *The Literary History of the American Revolution, 1763–1783.* New York: Barnes & Noble, 1941.

Van Tyne, Claude H. *The Causes of the War of Independence.* Houghton Mifflin Co., 1922.

Van Tyne, Claude H. *England and America, Rivals in the American Revolution.* New York: Macmillan Co., 1927.

Winslow, Ola Elizabeth. *Meetinghouse Hill, 1630–1783.* New York: W. W. Norton & Co. 1972.

Wood, Gordon S. *Creation of the American Republic.* Durham, N.C.: University of North Carolina Press, 1969.